A PASTORAL
REVOLUTION

BY GUIDO VIGNELLI

A PASTORAL
REVOLUTION

Six Talismanic Words In the
Ecclesial Debate on the Family

TRANSLATED BY JOSÉ A. SCHELINI

**The American Society for the
Defense of Tradition, Family, Property—TFP**

Original Italian edition
Copyright © 2016 Tradizione Famiglia Proprietà
Anno 22, n. 70, 2016
Director: Julio Loredo
Management, Administration, and Editorial:
Tradizione Famiglia Proprietà, Viale Liegi, 44 – 00198 Roma
Tel. 06/8417603 – Email: info@atfp.it – Web: www.atfp.it

Italian TFP – Italian edition: 4,000 copies
Italian TFP – first English edition: 1,000 copies
American TFP – second English edition

ISBN: 978-1-877905-54-4 (paperback)
ISBN: 978-1-877905-15-5 (e-book)
Library of Congress Control Number: 2018954323

Printed in the United States of America

Contents

Publisher's Foreword

On April 18, 2005, in his homily for the Mass "Pro Eligendo Romano Pontifice" before the Conclave that would elevate him to the Papacy, Joseph Cardinal Ratzinger warned of a "dictatorship of relativism." Today, years after these warnings, relativism's threat to the Faith has only increased.

Not satisfied with silencing the voice of Faith in the public square, the dictatorship of relativism aims to change the Church's unchangeable dogmatic and moral doctrines. It thus has the support of neo-modernists, who claim that Jesus' clear words simply reflect the culture of His time, whereas today, the Savior's commands must be reinterpreted to suit our very different culture.

These anti-apostles subscribe to the erroneous beliefs that Truth evolves and that official Revelation did not end with the death of the last Apostle but rather that God continuously reveals Himself through culture and history. Building on these false premises, neo-modernists argue that the Church must follow the "signs of the times," and welcome contraception and cohabitation, divorce and adulterous "remarriage," same-sex couples and transgenderism.

As heresies have plagued the Church from the beginning, the subversive efforts of neo-modernists would not normally surprise us. However, there are two aggravating factors: The great number of neo-modernists in the Church, and their unquestioned ability to deceive and move large sectors of the faithful from Truth to error.

In *A Pastoral Revolution*, Guido Vignelli zeroes in on one of the standard techniques used by neo-modernists to change the Church. It consists of their manipulative use of the flexible meaning of words or catch phrases that results in shifting people from the Church's traditional morality to a sinful opposite. He bases himself on *Unperceived Ideological Transshipment and Dialogue*, the 1965 masterly study by Prof. Plinio Corrêa de Oliveira—founder of the Brazilian Society for the Defense of Tradition, Family, and Property (TFP) and inspirer of autonomous sister TFPs and like-minded organizations around the world.

Dialogue's author called these targeted catch phrases "talismanic" words since they have an almost magical attraction. He cited words like *dialogue* and *peace* as examples. Vignelli updates this concept by examining terms used in the Church today. Thus, he analyzes the traditional and new meanings of six talismanic words—*pastoral, mercy, listening, discernment, accompaniment*, and *integration*—and how the faithful are imperceptibly led from the original correct understanding to another that is erroneous.

It is a diabolically clever process. No one is more interested in confusing the faithful than Satan. He has always drawn people away from the truths of the Faith. In the Savior's words, "[Satan] was a murderer from the beginning and does not stand in truth, because there is no truth in him. When he tells a lie, he speaks in character, because he is a liar and the father of lies" (John 8:44).

Unperceived ideological transshipment is not the only subterfuge neo-modernists use. The TFP founder also denounced another technique: When the Church's enemies target a Catholic truth for destruction, they first silence and hide it. They try to erase all memory of it. For a long time, the truth goes unmentioned; its raison d'être unexplored; its perfections unexpounded; its ordered beauty consigned to oblivion; its conformity to God's plan untaught. After inducing this universal amnesia, the enemies of the Church then move in for the assault. Their attack finds the truth's defenders unprepared, disorganized, and unsure of the importance of what is at stake.

Have we not seen this happen to the sacrament of marriage and the Christian family over the last half-century since the Second Vatican Council? Has the Church's authentic and solid teaching on both sacred institutions not been forgotten by many who still call themselves Catholic? Why do we see a depressingly high number of annulments being issued today?

The main culprit is the neglect of Church teaching. It paves the way for the changing of people's attitudes through these talismanic words. The results are devastating. For example, a 2016 Pew Research Center poll reports that a mere 13% of Catholics who still attend weekly Mass (a far cry from 1955's seventy-five percent rate for Sunday Mass attendance[1]) believe contraception to be morally wrong. Forty-five percent responded that contraception is morally acceptable, while 42% believed that it was not a moral issue.[2]

Should such crass ignorance about the intrinsic evil of contraception not trigger frequent sermons instructing the faithful on the sinfulness of contraception, and the everlasting fires of Hell God created and reserved for those who die in the state of mortal sin? There should

---

1. Lydia Saad, "Catholics' Church Attendance Resumes Downward Slide," *Gallup.com*, Apr. 9, 2018, http://news.gallup.com/poll/232226/church-attendance -among-catholics-resumes-downward-slide.aspx.

2. "Where the Public Stands on Religious Liberty vs. Nondiscrimination," no. 4. Pew Research Center, Sept. 28, 2016, http://www.pewforum.org/2016/09/28/ 4-very-few-americans-see-contraception-as-morally-wrong/.

be sermons emphasizing marriage's primary function—the bearing and educating of children—and that mutual spousal support is the secondary one.

Tragically, the process of doctrinal and moral trans-shipment denounced in this booklet has caused confusion in millions of Catholic souls. Barely a thread of Faith remains in such souls. Adapting a metaphor used by the TFP founder, such souls are like a flask of exquisite perfume (where the perfume is the Faith), which was negligently left open, and forgotten. Due to this oversight the precious contents ever so slowly evaporate, leaving the bottle empty. The label is still glued to the outside of the perfume bottle, but the flask is bone-dry within, ready to be filled with some other liquid. This devastated wasteland is the perfect moral environment for neo-modernists to implement their Pastoral Revolution.

Guido Vignelli's study aims to raise awareness among shepherds and faithful to the grave danger menacing the City of God. The technique he denounces is efficacious in leading many of the faithful astray. Souls must be warned and prepared against this neo-modernist assault. For everyone who loves Our Lord, His Blessed Mother, and the Church, there is no time to lose. There are wolves within the sheepfold, many in sheep's clothing, and we must defend the Lord's Flock.

Spring Grove, Penn., May 13, 2018
Raymond E. Drake
President

Preface

This book is intended as a tool to clarify family issues in the modern world. For this end, we will intervene in the confused debate generated by the first Synod on the Family (October 5–19, 2014), and which grew during and since the second (October 4–25, 2015).

This essay examines some keywords launched or relaunched by the post-synodal debate and widely disseminated by the media. We wonder if this phenomenon corresponds to the *pastoral conversion of ecclesial language* augured by the Synod. They are in fact ambivalent words or buzzwords that can be misinterpreted and are likely not only to confuse Christian public opinion further, but also lead it astray in a permissive sense, eventually diverting all ecclesial life toward relativism, and, consequently, the civil sphere as well.

It seems necessary, therefore, that such keywords, rather than being taken for granted, be indeed examined in their original and correct meaning, and compared with the new and distorted sense employed in the post-synodal debate. Those words, which we call *talismanic,* risk becoming tools of a psychological propaganda ploy called *unperceived ideological transshipment,* intended precisely to transship the faithful from a true to a false position. For a more profound understanding of this technique, please read the summary of Prof. Plinio Corrêa de Oliveira's 1965 essay, *Unperceived Ideological Transshipment and Dialogue* in the appendix.[3]

---

3. See Plinio Corrêa de Oliveira, *Unperceived Ideological Transshipment and Dialogue*, Oct. 1, 1982, http://www.tfp.org/tfp-home/books/unperceived-ideological-transshipment-and-dialogue.html.

This book was written shortly before the publication of Pope Francis's Apostolic Exhortation *Amoris Laetitia*. No changes were made to it though as we believe its analysis remains valid.

We place this work in the hands of the Blessed Virgin Mary, asking her to deign to use it as a tool to prevent non-Catholic thinking and practice from prevailing in the Church, as Pope Paul VI famously mentioned, and to pave the way for the coming Reign of her Immaculate Heart, as she promised at Fatima, exactly one hundred years ago.

INTRODUCTION
Words Flying in the Wind

The conclusions of the latest General Assemblies of Synod of Bishops on marriage and family, held in 2014 and 2015, resulted from a compromise that has raised many concerns. However, the study of those assemblies remains important because they proposed a new orientation for the Church on how to diagnose and treat the current ills of family life. Moreover, their approach tends to involve everything Christian and will thus have an ever greater influence in the life of the Church and, consequently, in the temporal sphere.

For one, "the mystery of God's love for men and women, receives its linguistic form from the vocabulary of marriage and the family."[4] Therefore the way we think and live our marriage and family roles highly affects the way we think and live about God, Jesus Christ, the Church, and the Sacraments; an ambiguity or error in the former may have grave consequences on the latter.

It should be noted that this synodal orientation was expressed not so much by syllogistic reasoning as by employing keywords widely seen in the media. Today they are applied to problems examined and to solutions proposed using correlative maxims, formulas, and slogans that suggest a reform of Church practice.

It is no wonder that in today's Church one speaks, writes, and teaches with keywords, slogans, and soundbites. We live in the communication society, and since the

---

4. Benedict XVI, "Address of His Holiness Benedict XVI to the Participants in the Ecclesial Diocesan Convention of Rome," Jun. 6, 2005, http://w2.vatican.va/content /benedict-xvi/en/speeches/2005/june/documents/hf_ben-xvi_spe_20050606 _convegno-famiglia.html.

Second Vatican Council there has been much insistence that the Church evangelize using modern rules of communication.

The duty remains, however, to use words carefully because, as is known, they spread ideas which later inspire actions so that today's language can become tomorrow's thought, which in turn can give rise to customs the day after tomorrow. Moreover, the more beautiful words are, the more dangerous they can become, as improper use may cause them to be misunderstood and placed at the service of deception: "For they shall sow wind, and reap a whirlwind" (Osee 8:7). Furthermore, "many have fallen by the edge of the sword, but not so many as have perished by their own tongue" (Ecclus. 28:22).

Towards the end of his pontificate, Paul VI confided this concern to his friend Jean Guitton: "A kind of non-Catholic thinking seems to dominate at times within Catholicism, and tomorrow this non-Catholic thinking may prevail."[5]

Now then, today there is a danger that non-Catholic thought becomes precisely the strongest and manages to prevail in a confused and weakened Church. This is obtained not so much by spreading errors but rather ambiguous and slippery words that, while having a Christian origin, are seized upon and manipulated by anti-Christian culture and spread in Catholic circles to contaminate and prepare them to give in and surrender to the enemy. If this is true, then current ecclesial language poses a problem, not only of form but also substance.

It seems necessary, therefore, to examine the Synod's

---

5. Jean Guitton, *Paul VI segreto* (Cinisello Balsamo, Italy: Ed. San Paolo, 2002), 153.

keywords in their meaning, scope, and influence. Above all we must consider them not so much in their proper sense—as found in the dictionary and used in everyday language—but in the derived sense employed in the contextual language that has been wittily called *ecclesialese* or *clericalese*.

In fact, as we shall see, while such words are legitimate and of ancient origin, once inserted into the ecclesiastical language they gradually take on a new and improper meaning in practice which is sometimes opposed to the initial one.

This semantic evolution produces a significant result: Persons employing those words are gradually *transshipped* from a precise idea or position (let us call it white), first to an ambiguous (gray) stance and then to an opposite (black) position. For example, the use of certain words can push the user to replace a global judgment with a partial one, a substantial judgment with an accidental one, or a moral judgment with a sentimental one. One thus ends up considering good or at least tolerable what at first was deemed bad—or vice versa.[6]

These keywords are not used in a restrained way to express what they mean—a concept, value, or judgment that can easily be accepted or rejected by an alert listener—but tend to achieve what they mean, i.e. to produce an effect (making a choice, taking a position, or adopting a behavior) on those using them. In turn, users find it difficult not to accept the keyword's effect, for it influences them in a particular direction. Magic formulas

---

6. See Aldo di Cillo Pagotto, Robert F. Vasa, and Athanasius Schneider, *Preferential Option for the Family: One Hundred Questions and Answers Relating to the Synod* (Rome: Edizioni Supplica Filiale, 2015), chap. 11, http://www.tfp.org/images /stories/PDF_files/Preferential_Option_for_the_Family_English.pdf.

operate in a similar way, and that is why such keywords can be called *magic* or *talismanic* (see box). While seemingly trivial and innocuous, in the slanted sense given them, these keywords can exert a dangerous influence, by tending to manipulate their users' mindset through an implicit technique of psychological persuasion.

Therefore, while one should not demonize the keywords in the synodal debate we will examine, neither should one accept them uncritically. It seems important, therefore, to analyze them carefully to reveal the meaning they are being given and hinder their profound in-

---

The Talismanic Word

This is a word whose legitimate meaning is congenial and, at times, even noble; but it is also a word that has some elasticity. When it is used tendentiously, it begins to shine with a new radiance, fascinating the patient and taking him much farther than he could have imagined.

Twisted out of shape and distorted, wholesome and even dignified words have been used to label a number of mistakes, errors and blunders. We could even say that the effects of this technique are more harmful when the word being abused is more elevated and dignified—*corruptio optimi pessima*. Some words with a dignified connotation that have been transformed into deceitful talismans and placed at the service of error are: social justice, ecumenism, dialogue, peace, irenicism, and coexistence.

Plinio Corrêa de Oliveira, *Unperceived Ideological Transshipment and Dialogue*, ch. 3, 2C.

fluence on unsuspecting minds.

This influence is possible because in expressing a weak thought *talismanic words* are also weak. Their power lies in their ability to psychologically seduce, in the context in which they are used. Accordingly, in order to break their spell, it suffices to recall their actual meaning, subjecting them to the light of reason and faith. Then their *magic* quickly vanishes, like a ghost, when observed with a watchful eye by people unafraid of becoming its victims: "Such realistic reminders of what's what can serve as a form of 'exorcism,' as can the corrective irony of sober language."[7]

According to authoritative protagonists and observers, the dominant keywords in the synodal discussion were: *pastoral, mercy, listening, discernment, accompaniment, integration.* In fact, these words occur very often in the Synod's official documents: *pastoral* 90 times; *mercy* 48; *discernment* 45; *accompaniment* 102. *Integration* occurs only 24 times, but when we add the word it presupposes, namely, *welcome*, which is repeated 74 times, the combined total is 98 times.[8] Other recurring words such as *complexity, deepening, challenge* do not seem to have the importance of those first mentioned. In contrast, the keyword *sin* is found only three times in the synodal documents.

Let us examine one keyword at a time, considering it in itself and its relationships. As we shall see, the first two words (*pastoral* and *mercy*) guide the others.

---

7. Josef Pieper, *Faith Hope Love* (San Francisco: Ignatius Press, 1997), 271.

8. See Antonio Spadaro, *La famiglia oltre il miraggio: Tutti i documenti del Sinodo straordinario 2015* (Milan-Rome: Ancora/La Civiltà Cattolica, 2015), 29.

CHAPTER 1

Pastoral

The New Ecclesial Strategy

Pastoral has become the dominant keyword in ecclesial language. Indeed it appears to sum up the essence of Christianity. Everything is conceived, designed, and achieved in its name.

What Is Pastoral?

In its proper sense, pastoral relates to a shepherd's grazing activities: guiding, feeding, and protecting his flock from wolves. In the religious sense, it is the art of governing the faithful, exercised by the bishop as pastor of souls; it is the doctrine that describes and regulates the tasks of the priestly office.

The pastoral ministry is oriented to the glory to God, the salvation of souls, and the good of the Church. Indeed, pastors "therefore, should not only encourage the faithful to seek this happiness but should frequently remind them that the sure way of obtaining it is to possess the virtues of faith and charity."[9] In short, pastoral policy is the supreme art of governing souls, regulated by the supernatural virtue of prudence.[10]

Pastoral theology is a practical science that studies how to adjust human life to the requirements of revealed

---

9. *The Catechism of the Council of Trent*, art. XII "And life everlasting," accessed Mar. 5, 2017, http://www.catholicbook.com/AgredaCD/Trent/tcreed12.htm.

10. See St. Gregory the Great, *Pastoral Care*, trans. James Barmby in *Nicene and Post-Nicene Fathers*, 2nd Series, vol. 12, ed. Philip Schaff and Henry Wace (Buffalo, NY: Christian Literature Publishing Co., 1895), intro., rev. and ed. Kevin Knight for New Advent, http://www.newadvent.org/fathers/36011.htm.

Truth by fulfilling its dogmatic, moral, and liturgical principles. It does not address the goal but only the way to attain it by effectively announcing and transmitting the Gospel to humanity in a way that befits the opportunities of time and place.

Pastoral policy, therefore, depends on dogma, morality, and liturgy; it does not touch on the essence and foundation of the Church and cannot change dogmas, laws, and worship; it does not deal with *quod* (the thing) nor with *quia* (the reason why), but only with *quomodo* (how), that is to say, how to deal with rules, methods, and means of apostolate. Its relative autonomy of action is subordinated to the goal being pursued, namely the salvation of souls.

What Is Meant by Pastoral Today?

In current ecclesiastical language, the word pastoral tends to gradually take on a different meaning and a much broader scope which unveil its possibly *talismanic* role.

In a first stage, pastoral is no longer understood as the art of evangelization and Church government but as the supreme rule of Christianity in all its dimensions: dogmatic, moral, liturgical, and canonical. Therefore, every truth and law is admissible only insofar as it is compatible with the supreme requirements of pastoral policy.

Thus, a new pastoral policy is born, one that is understood not as the art of converting men to God by welcoming them in the Church, but as a pedagogy of dialogue and encounter among equals between the Church and humanity in its concrete historical and social situation, in order to achieve universal peace together. This is done in the name of a Christian realism which would impose a compromise between passively enduring the world and irresponsibly rejecting it.

In a second stage, pastoral policy takes a step forward and becomes the art of adapting the Church to the needs of modernity, by inserting it into both history, as the latter unfolds, and the evolution of the cosmos. For example, pastoral policy is supposedly endowed with the prophetic mission of adapting social and family realities to the present anthropological mutation.

At the end of this process, a reversal takes place: Instead of adapting life to truth, truth is adapted to life, and therefore pastoral policy is no longer a way but a goal, not a means but an end. As a result, the evolution of pastoral policy as a talismanic word is likely to trans-ship the faithful from Christianity to a secularized humanism: No longer God first, but man.

This new pastoral is carried out according to subsequent guidance expressed by several well-known slogans, which we will examine.

Primacy of Pastoral Policy Over Doctrine

In assuming that life holds precedence over truth, the way over the goal, and the means over the end, modern theology ends up enshrining the *primacy of pastoral policy over doctrine*. Sometimes it does this by affirming the importance of research and of the doubts that supposedly motivate it.

In a first phase, this slogan is used with the pretext of bringing doctrine closer to pastoral activities, thus reducing the former to an *a posteriori* justification of the latter. Consequently, freed from its dependence on doctrine the new pastoral policy ends up subjecting doctrine to the requirements of transforming practices. Here, then, theory no longer precedes practice but on the contrary, practice precedes theory, and orthodoxy becomes dependent on *orthopraxis,* a word purposely revived by liberation theologians who support this trend.

In a second phase, this pastoral policy no longer restricts itself to subduing doctrine but replaces it. Indeed, many well-known theologians argue that after the Second Vatican Council, truth and laws should be replaced by pastoral values and norms. Therefore, pastoral policy is no longer based on dogmatic, moral, and legal foundations but existential, psychological, and community issues. Indeed, theology itself should become existential ecclesiology, in other words, a pastoral practice that implements the so-called reform of the Church as required by the needs of modern man.

For example, the traditional moral teaching on sexuality, marriage, and family is now assumed to be contradicted not only by the behavior of many of the faithful, which is a fact, but also by the needs of pastoral projects, which raises a question of law. To resolve this contradiction, they do not propose to adapt the fact to the law, but the law to the fact, that is, to adapt moral doctrine to the practice of the Church's grassroots. In this sense, behavior becomes the absolute criterion and supreme law not only of life but also of Church doctrine and teaching, replacing her magisterial function with the pastoral one.

At the end of the process, "the only true *orthodoxy* is . . . *orthopraxy*," as a future Pope denounced in his time.[11] Dogma, morals, and apostolate are gradually being replaced by good sentiments, pastoral projects,

---

11. Joseph Cardinal Ratzinger with Vittorio Messori, *The Ratzinger Report: An Exclusive Interview on the State of the Church*, trans. Salvator Attanasio and Graham Harrison (San Francisco: Ignatius Press, 1985), 185.

and ecclesial animations, so that "there is no longer a need for miracles just read the owner's manual," as Kierkegaard quipped.

Accordingly, the Magisterium of the Church risks ending up relativized through subjection to the requirements of pastoral practice. This pragmatism is an application of the Modernist axiom that *truth is thought adapted to life*, and justice is the adaptation of the will to situations and customs; this will also end up applying the revolutionary axiom that a theory's criterion of validity is reduced to its practical result, and thus man's task is not to understand reality but to transform it.[12]

Doctrine and Practice

The Gospel teaches that the Church must not only be a loving Mother but also and above all the authoritative Teacher of transcendent and supernatural Divine truth, fulfilling the mission of instructing the ignorant, advising the doubtful, and admonishing sinners as commanded by the Holy Spirit. In so doing the Church imitates Jesus Christ as Master by transmitting the salvific doctrine He taught:

> And Jesus going out saw a great multitude: and he had compassion on them, because they were as sheep not having a shepherd, and he began to *teach* them many things [about the Kingdom of God] (Mark: 6:34).
>
> And they were astonished at his doctrine. For he was *teaching* them as one having power (Mark 1:22).
>
> Whosoever revolts, and continues not in the

---

12. See Karl Marx, *Theses on Feuerbach*, accessed Mar. 14, 2017, https://msuweb.montclair.edu/~furrg/gned/marxtonf45.pdf.

doctrine of Christ, has not God. He that continues in the *doctrine*, the same has both the Father and the Son. If any man come to you, and bring not this *doctrine*, receive him not into the house nor say to him, God speed you. For he that says unto him, God speed you, communicates with his wicked works (2 John 9–11).

Pastoral practice can never be separated from doctrinal truth. Just as the body cannot be separated from the soul that forms it, so also pastoral policy cannot be separated from the doctrine that establishes and justifies it. As a result, a substantial change in pastoral policy can gradually bring about, at least implicitly, a change in doctrine with serious and easily predictable consequences. In short, the practice of good and the knowledge of truth should enrich each other; goodness needs truth as evil needs error. Hence the Church must adopt a pastoral policy of truth:

> The good of the person lies in being in the Truth and doing the Truth.[13]

> The pastoral policy of truth can hurt and be uncomfortable. But it is the way to healing, peace, and interior freedom. A pastoral policy that truly seeks to help people must always be based on the truth; only what is true can ultimately be pastoral.[14]

---

13. John Paul II, "Speech to the Participants of the International Congress on Moral Theology," Apr. 10, 1986, no. 1, http://w2.vatican.va/content/john-paul-ii/it/speeches/1986/april/documents/hf_jp-ii_spe_19860410_teologia-morale.html.

14. Benedict XVI, "La pastorale del matrimonio deve fondarsi sulla verità," *Osservatore Romano,* Nov. 30, 2011, http://www.osservatoreromano.va/it/news/la-pastorale-del-matrimonio-deve-fondarsi-sulla-ve.

> Pastoral policy has become intrusive to the
> point of absorbing all other disciplines of sa-
> cred doctrine.... Pastoral theology itself has
> become pastoral policy, i.e. it has lost the cri-
> teria that bound it to theology, cutting the
> last ties that made it depend on eternal
> Truth.... Pastoral policy thus remains con-
> ditioned to psychology, sociology, history,
> etc. but it is no longer theology subject to the
> principles of faith.[15]

Moreover, there is no such thing as doctrinally neutral practice; all praxis presupposes a theological or
philosophical theory, a vision of man, society, and history. The very concept of practice requires a good to
achieve, i.e. an ideal to translate into action, a role
model, so that a practice is valid only if it achieves its established goal.

Primacy of Conscience Over Law
If life takes precedence over truth, the means over the
end, and pastoral policy over doctrine, then the new theology consequently enshrines the *primacy of conscience
over the Law*. But this maxim too risks assuming a talismanic value.

Here we need to establish a distinction between the
traditional meaning of *conscience* and the modern and
talismanic sense it has been taking on in contemporary
theology.

The traditional meaning of conscience can be understood on more than one level. At the theological
level, it is the judgment that a person makes about the

---

15. Enrico Zoffoli C.P., *Dizionario del Cristianesimo* (Rome: Synopsis, 1992), 380.

compliance of his actions with God's Law and Christian legislation.

> Conscience is like God's herald and messenger; it does not command things on its own authority, but commands them as coming from God's authority, like a herald when he proclaims the edict of the king. This is why conscience has binding force.[16]

> Of itself, conscience is not an arbiter of the moral actions that it suggests. One's conscience is the interpreter of an inner and higher standard; it did not create itself. . . . It is the subjective and immediate intimation by a law which we must call natural, although many people today do not want to hear about natural law.[17]

In modern thought, however, conscience is understood as a feeling which gives the subject self-assurance to claim to be able to know and judge for himself infallibly. In this case, conscience is no longer the voice of God or Divine Law, indeed not even of an abstract truth or justice, but only self-rule, a sort of idol to whom all is permitted and to whom everything must be sacrificed. Today one seems to be back in the days of the Greek poet Menander, who said that "conscience is a god to all mortals."[18]

---

16. St. Bonaventure, *In Secundum Librum Sententiarum*, in *Doctoris seraphici S. Bonaventurae Opera Omnia*, Vol. II (Florence: Typographia Collegii S. Bonaventurae, 1885), dist. 39, a. 1, q. 3, http://www.archive.org/stream/doctorisseraphic 02bona#page/906/mode/2up.

17. Paul VI, General Audience, Feb. 12, 1969, http://w2.vatican.va/content /paul-vi/it/audiences/1969/documents/hf_p-vi_aud_19690212.html.

18. Menander of Athens, *Monosticha 564* quoted in W. Gurney Benham, *Cassell's Book of Quotations*, rev. ed. (New York: Cassell and Company, Ltd, 1914), 469.

Therefore, such conscience has no need to be upright, that is, rightly formed and just. It suffices that it be authentic, in other words, sincere and spontaneous and not influenced by anything outside itself, not even the demands of truth, goodness, and justice. This authenticity is understood merely as the person's consistency with himself. Hence it is a subjective and emotional conscience that justifies "freedom as an opportunity for the flesh" (Gal. 5:13),[19] i.e. as slaves of disordered passions. "The cultural tendencies. . . in which freedom and law are set in opposition to each other and kept apart, and freedom is exalted almost to the point of idolatry—lead to a *'creative' understanding of moral conscience*, which diverges from the teaching of the Church's tradition and her Magisterium."[20]

This modern, secular misconception of conscience has penetrated Church environments and plays a talismanic role by gradually changing not only the relationship between conscience, truth, and law but also the very meaning of conscience.

In a first stage, current theology attempts to discredit the true meaning of conscience. Indeed, it is claimed that traditional doctrine has reduced conscience to applying abstract moral laws to concrete, real life cases without grasping the uniqueness of people in their situations. So they argue that moral laws are not so much a binding objective criterion for judgments of conscience, but rather a background for the conscience to act on; and its decisions are not bound to comply with norms,

---

19. New American Bible Revised Edition (henceforth "NABRE").

20. John Paul II, Encyclical *Veritatis Splendor*, Aug. 6, 1993, no. 54, http://w2.vatican.va/content/john-paul-ii/en/encyclicals/documents/hf_jp -ii_enc_06081993_veritatis-splendor.html.

as these serve only as general guidance to be creatively applied depending on the case.

Accordingly, the moral conscience should provide an existential evaluation of concrete situations to make decisions that elude moral laws by way of exceptions. In short, the creative conscience would be entitled to find pastoral solutions contrary not only to the ecclesiastical Magisterium but also to Divine Law. Nor would the Moral Law and the Magisterium have any right to be obeyed by an authentic conscience. The Church thus ceases to be the *morum regula* (Saint Augustine), and her laws and judgments only have a relative value. The result is that following behind the dogmatic Magisterium, the moral Magisterium too risks becoming neutralized.

In a second stage, the new pastoral practice goes a step further by establishing the *primacy of conscience over Law*: not only over ecclesiastical rules but also over Divine Law. Indeed, if laws have been replaced by existential requirements, then the moral Law now depends on the conscience, that is, on being known and consented to by an individual or, ultimately, a community. Actions that are evil *per se* or *states* of sin no longer exist, but only actions and situations that one's conscience evaluates according to temporal and spatial criteria.

At the end of this process, the primacy of conscience over Law leads to *replacing the Law with the now idolized conscience*. As a result, the moral imperative of conscience is no longer expressed by the old saying, "become who you are,"[21] that is, accomplish your mission in the nature and role that God gave you, but rather *be*

---

21. Pindar, *Pythian II*, 70, trans. and ed. by Diane Arnson Svarlien, from *The Odes of Pindar*, in Perseus Project 1.0 (New Haven: Yale University Press, 1991), http://www.perseus.tufts.edu.

what you become, in other words, *adjust to your aspirations and desires.* The lack of immutable criteria ends up rendering decisions of conscience arbitrary.

Moral Law and Conscience

In fact, conscience is not a mere sentiment someone passively suffers under the imposition of existential needs but a practical judgment actively expressed and based on reasoning (see. Rom. 2:15). Therefore, just as freedom and truth, conscience and the moral law are neither contradictory nor in competition, as the two greatest apostles of charity, Saints John and Paul teach:

> Whoever says, "I know him," but does not keep his commandments is a liar, and the truth is not in him (1 John 2:4–NABRE).
>
> Therefore, whoever disregards this, disregards not a human being but God, who [also] gives his Holy Spirit to you (1 Thes. 4:8–NABRE).
>
> Similarly, an athlete cannot receive the winner's crown except by competing according to the rules (2 Tim. 2:5–NABRE).

The Magisterium of the Church confirms it:

> A false philosophy teaches us to despise and reject the objective norm, i.e. the Law, as something foreign to the true being, as an enemy that dissolves the fertility and strength of life. Here we see the danger of this philosophy for the sanctity of customs in marriage and the family. Therefore, it is necessary to teach man, who yearns for temporal and eternal

happiness, that both can only be found in the bond of duty and the Law of God. . . . Wishing to free man from the constraint of the Divine order by appealing to a God-given freedom is a self-contradiction. . . . It is fatal both for the Church and for human society when pastors of souls, in teaching and practice, habitually and almost on principle keep silent when the laws established by God, always valid in every case, are violated in married life.[22]

Freedom of conscience is never freedom "from" the truth but always and only freedom "in" the truth. . . . The Church puts herself always and only at the *service of conscience*, helping it to avoid being tossed to and fro by every wind of doctrine proposed by human deceit (see Eph. 4:14), and helping it not to swerve from the truth about the good of man, but rather, especially in more difficult questions, to attain the truth with certainty and to abide in it.[23]

An attempt is made to legitimize so-called "pastoral" solutions contrary to the teaching of the Magisterium, and to justify a "creative" hermeneutic according to which the moral conscience is in no way obliged, in every case, by a particular negative precept.

No one can fail to realize that these approaches pose a challenge to the *very identity*

---

22. Pius XII, "Speech to the Cardinals and Bishops in Rome for the Proclamation of the Dogma of the Assumption of the Blessed Virgin Mary," Nov. 2, 1950, http://w2.vatican.va/content/pius-xii/la/speeches/1950/documents/hf_p-xii_spe_19501102_episcopato-mondo-cattolico.html.

23. John Paul II, *Veritatis splendor*, no. 64.

of the moral conscience in relation to human freedom and God's law.[24]

In the field of conjugal morality the Church is Teacher and Mother and acts as such.

As Teacher, she never tires of proclaiming the moral norm that must guide the responsible transmission of life. The Church is in no way the author or the arbiter of this norm. In obedience to the truth which is Christ . . . the Church interprets the moral norm and proposes it to all people of good will, without concealing its demands of radicalness and perfection.

As Mother, the Church is close to the many married couples who find themselves in difficulty over this important point of the moral life. . . .

The Church never ceases to exhort and encourage all to resolve whatever conjugal difficulties may arise without ever falsifying or compromising the truth. . . . Accordingly, the concrete pedagogy of the Church must always remain linked with her doctrine and never be separated from it. . . . "To diminish in no way the saving teaching of Christ constitutes an eminent form of charity for souls."[25]

Pastoral Inculturation

While the new pastoral policy presupposes the primacy of conscience over doctrine and law, in the social sphere it

---

24. Ibid., no. 56.

25. John Paul II, Apostolic Exhortation *Familiaris consortio*, Nov. 22, 1981, no. 33, http://w2.vatican.va/content/john-paul-ii/en/apost_exhortations/documents /hf_jp-ii_exh_19811122_familiaris-consortio.html.

promotes a *pastoral inculturation* which enshrines the primacy of conscience and collective culture over truth and evangelical law.

Currently, by definition, *inculturation* means a process by which one becomes a member of the surrounding culture.[26] In the ecclesial sphere it "means the intimate transformation of authentic cultural values through their integration in Christianity and the insertion of Christianity in the various human cultures."[27] Inculturation thus has two aspects: It is "the incarnation of the Gospel in native cultures and also the introduction of these cultures into the life of the Church."[28] It is a methodology that evaluates and purifies the wealth of local cultures to put them at the service of evangelization so as to build a Christian civilization.

In the new pastoral policy, however, inculturation can assume a talismanic meaning. It is not limited to being a missionary methodology aiming to evangelize but becomes a new concept of evangelization itself, which is in fact reduced to adapting the Gospel to indigenous cultures. Inculturation then ceases to be a tool to evangelize

---

26. [Ed.—Regretfully, the word *inculturation* is imprecise and prone to misinterpretation. During its 2,000 years history, the Church has absorbed certain good elements from specific cultures, for example, the chasuble or the faldstool used by a bishop during a Pontifical Mass. While enriching Church life, these elements never altered her perennial teaching on faith and morals. On the other hand, it is proper to the Catholic faith to inform culture and civilization so that these reflect the Gospel principles, and the Church has always done this. See Plinio Corrêa de Oliveira, *Revolution and Counter-Revolution*, part 1, ch. 7, 2B.]

27. John Paul II, Encyclical *Redemptoris Missio*, Dec. 7, 1990, no. 52, http://w2.vatican.va/content/john-paul-ii/en/encyclicals/documents /hf_jp-ii_enc_07121990_redemptoris-missio.html.

28. John Paul II, Encyclical *Slavorum apostoli*, Jun. 2, 1985, no. 21, http://w2.vatican.va/content/john-paul-ii/en/encyclicals/documents /hf_jp-ii_enc_19850602_slavorum-apostoli.html.

and ends up becoming the goal of evangelization.[29]

Since the new pastoral policy is understood as the adaptation of truth to the historical and social needs of humanity, it must vary with time and space. It cannot admit pre-established truths, immutable guidelines, rigid rules, and norms that impose ready-made solutions. Concretely, pastoral practice must adapt not only to historical and geographical contexts but also cultural and religious ones. Ecclesial doctrine and laws will have to conform to the customs of peoples, ethnic groups, and tribes even if they are, and remain, pagan.

This means that this inculturated pastoral risks falling into the old thesis of latitudinarianism, that is, reducing religion to an opinion and custom that changes according to geography: An error already condemned by the Church.[30]

> The Missionary is the Apostle of Jesus Christ. He does not have the task of transplanting specifically European civilization to mission lands, but to make those people, who sometimes have ancient cultures, ready and able to accept and assimilate the elements of Christian life and customs, which easily and naturally fit in with any healthy civilization and give it full capacity and strength to ensure and guarantee human dignity and happiness. Indigenous Catholics must be truly members of the family of God and citizens of His kingdom (see Eph. 2:19)

---

29. See Julien Ries, "Inculturazione," in Card. Paul Poupard, *Dizionario delle religioni* (Rome: Città Nuova, 2001), 1080.

30. See Pius IX, *Syllabus of Errors*, Dec. 8, 1864, props. 15-6, http://www.ewtn.com/library/PAPALDOC/P9SYLL.HTM.

without ceasing to be citizens of their earthly homeland.[31]

Evangelization risks losing its power and disappearing altogether if one empties or adulterates its content under the pretext of translating it; if, in other words, one sacrifices this reality and destroys the unity without which there is no universality, out of a wish to adapt a universal reality to a local situation.[32]

It is neither safe nor free from danger to speak of theologies that should be as numerous and different as are continents and human cultures. In fact, the content of the faith is either Catholic, or it is nothing.[33]

Pastoral Conversion of the Church

If life takes precedence over truth and if pastoral policy becomes the supreme criterion of Christianity, then you have to adapt not only evangelism but also the entire ecclesiastical order to the needs of time and place; this is why current theology calls for a *pastoral conversion of the Church*, which would be a talismanic solution. But the slogan we are examining talks about *conversion* with a very different meaning.

According to current theology, pastoral policy in the

31. Pius XII, "Speech to the Pontifical Mission Societies," Jun. 24, 1944, http://w2.vatican.va/content/pius-xii/it/speeches/1944/documents/hf_p-xii_spe_19440624_opere-missionarie.html.

32. Paul VI, Apostolic Exhortation *Evangelii nuntiandi*, Dec. 8, 1975, no. 63, http://w2.vatican.va/content/paul-vi/en/apost_exhortations/documents/hf_p-vi_exh_19751208_evangelii-nuntiandi.html.

33. Paul VI, "Closing Allocution for the III General Assembly of the Synod of Bishops," Oct. 26, 1974, http://w2.vatican.va/content/paul-vi/it/speeches/1974/documents/hf_p-vi_spe_19741026_allocuzione-finale.html.

past was reduced to a mere instrument intended not so much to save souls as to ensure ecclesial power. Today, however, the Church can no longer afford to *carry out* pastoral policy but must herself *become* pastoral work, dialogue, sharing, and participation, not only to the outside but also within.

In a first stage, this pastoral conversion implies that the requirements of present-day society have not only the power but also the right to force the ecclesiastical institution to discard privileges, exemptions, and rights outdated by history. Therefore, they argue that the Church should generously renounce all that and stop pursuing her own good and interests (even spiritual), to fulfill the needs of the modern world.

In a second stage, pastoral conversion goes further by demanding that the Church give up being a citadel or fortress closed to the world and earnestly undertake to level her ramparts and leave the ghetto to become a nomad's tent wandering in the desert of history. Of course, this can only be accomplished through a radical reform of Church structures in a pastoral and participatory way.

In a third stage, pastoral conversion demands that the Church also waive values hitherto considered nonnegotiable, including truths and laws revealed by God in Holy Scripture. In short, the idea is to ensure that dogma, morals, law, and liturgy are adapted to the needs of modern man. Curiously enough, current theology, which hardly speaks of any conversion of the world to the Church, sometimes explicitly speaks of this conversion of the Church to the world.

Accordingly, today's weak thought corresponds to a similarly weak pastoral policy that is not based on immutable truths but on psychological and sociological analyses that result in a practice committed to finding mediation solutions that end up in compromise. Indeed, pastoral policy is reduced to social psychotherapy not aimed at the cure of souls but of individual and social psyches. The result is that not only its methods and means but also its principles and values are not derived from Revelation but from modern human sciences (psychology, sociology, anthropology, etc.), which are given a sacred and almost *prophetic* value. This explains why the Church leadership, which in the past took the initiative anticipating problems and proposing solutions, today seems resigned to suffer the onslaught of its enemies, running after problems raised by modernity and offering compromise solutions.

In short, while they once insisted on ecclesial homogeneity and solidity, today they advocate a dynamic that sets the Church in motion and pushes her to get out of herself and tread the roads of the world. This requires not only a diversified but also diverging, decentralized, and thus fragmented, and possibly confrontational, ecclesial community.

However, a pastoral praxis which is not founded on truth and aimed at holiness looks like a sterile or counterproductive game. Moreover, it tends to become a consensus technique, inevitably influenced by individual or collective pressure from worldly powers.

This may result in serious consequences. Once the entire Religion is adapted to the supposed pastoral needs, ecclesial action is no longer guided by the light of Faith, animated by the fire of Charity, or regulated by the virtue of Prudence, but ends up surrendering to the chances of success to be had in complying with the demands of modernity. It is no longer a matter of "reestablishing all things in Christ" (Eph. 1:10) but only of rendering some vague service to humanity.

CHAPTER 2
Mercy
The Soul of the New Pastoral Policy

The main feature of the new pastoral policy, so central as to constitute its very soul, seems to be *mercy*, which is also why it is spoken of so wearily often today.

What Is Mercy?

By definition, to have mercy is to sympathize with the misery of others so as to help and remedy their situation. In God, mercy is an *ad extra* attribute and operation by which He succors people in misery and misfortune, giving them forgiveness and salvation. In Jesus Christ, mercy is the form assumed by Divine love to free man from sin and save him from evil: He is the Good Shepherd who nurtures, guides and protects the sheep, gathering them in His sheepfold (see John 15:10). In man, mercy is an active aspect of the moral virtue of charity.[34]

> Mercy is manifested in its true and proper aspect when it restores to value, promotes and draws good from all the forms of evil existing in the world and in man.[35]

> A person is said to be merciful [*misericors*], as being, so to speak, sorrowful at heart [*miserum cor*]; being affected with sorrow at

---

34. See Emile Janvier, OP, *Esposizione della morale cattolica* (Turin: Marietti, 1936), vol. 14, 179–89.

35. John Paul II, Encyclical *Dives in misericordia,* Nov. 30, 1980, no. 6, http://w2.vatican.va/content/john-paul-ii/en/encyclicals/documents /hf_jp-ii_enc_30111980_dives-in-misericordia.html.

the misery of another as though it were his
own.... And this is the effect of mercy. To sor-
row, therefore, over the misery of others belongs not to God; but it does most properly
belong to Him to dispel that misery, whatever
be the defect we call by that name.[36]

He has compassion on those who accept
his discipline, who are eager for his precepts
(Ecclus. 18:14–NABRE).

In the field of marriage, God's mercy has a well-
known symbolic application. In fact, in the Bible, it is re-
lated to God's unilateral fidelity to His marriage
covenant with His people by which He is willing to for-
give His Mystical Bride although she has committed the
sin of adultery by fornicating with unbelievers.[37] Similarly, a man or woman may be mercifully forgiven despite having sinned. In the family sphere, God's mercy is
expressed by the very indissolubility of the bond and the
respective rights and duties that bind the spouses to
each other and to their children to prevent them from
being left to the mercy of their whims and passions.

Therefore, how could mercy be shown for those who
not only do not condemn fornication as a fault but justify it as a need? And how can one not realize that a
mercy that justifies adultery or divorced-remarried cohabitation entails denying the true mercy due to the
innocent victims of these irregular family situations?
One is merciful when he undertakes to strengthen and

---

36. St. Thomas Aquinas, *Summa Theologiae*, trans. Fathers of the English Dominican Province (London: Burns and Oates, 1920) 1, q. 21, a. 3–rev. and ed. Kevin
Knight for New Advent, http://www.newadvent.org/summa/3060.htm.

37. See Jer. 2:22–37; Ezech. 16:15–63; Osee 2:4–15.

defend family ties and duties by making Christian couples understand their importance, rather than by loosening or dispensing them from their duties.

What Is Meant by Mercy Today?

While there is much talk of mercy in the Church today, it is all about its application. The clarification of its principles is neglected. Moreover, it is insinuated that mercy should be understood in a new meaning that was lost and is now rediscovered, an understanding that takes on a talismanic value.

In a first stage, advocates of the new pastoral policy criticize the rigid and so-called paternalistic practice of mercy that rebukes the sinner for his guilt and denies him pre-emptive pardon (always, in every case, and everywhere) without the necessary conditions for absolution: confession of sins, sincere repentance, resolve to sin no more, and atoning penance.

In a second stage, the new pastoral policy goes further and ends up becoming merciful not only with the sinner but also with sin, which is more excused than forgiven. Therefore, one is not limited to "hating the sin but loving the sinner" as Saint Augustine teaches,[38] but goes so far as to justify sin and absolve unrepentant sinners.

Writing against impunity for sin, Saint Augustine condemns those Christians who "hold out false hopes of impunity to their own depraved lives by means of this quasi compassion of God to the whole race."[39] Such

---

38. "With due love for the persons and hatred of the sin." St. Augustine, Letter 211, trans. J.G. Cunningham, in *Nicene and Post-Nicene Fathers,* 1st Series, vol. 1, ed. Philip Schaff, (Buffalo, NY: Christian Literature Publishing Co., 1887), rev. and ed. Kevin Knight for New Advent, http://www.newadvent.org/fathers/1102211.htm.

39. St. Augustine, *The City of God*, trans. Marcus Dods, in *Nicene and Post-Nicene Fathers*, 1st Series, vol. 2, ed. Philip Schaff (Buffalo, NY: Christian Literature Publishing Co., 1887), bk. 21, ch. 18, rev. and ed. Kevin Knight for New Advent, http://www.newadvent.org/fathers/120121.htm.

permissiveness is incompatible with the Divine goodness, which does not "permit sinful man to be deceived by those who claim to love him by justifying his sin."[40]

For example, regarding married life, "They are destroying mutual fidelity, who think that the ideas and morality of our present time concerning a certain harmful and false friendship with a third party can be countenanced, and who teach that a greater freedom of feeling and action in such external relations should be allowed to man and wife."[41]

Now let us see some maxims with which the new pastoral policy misunderstands the word *mercy*, revealing its implied talismanic role.

Maxims of False Mercy

A soft, sentimental, and pacifist feeling predominates today which promotes a mindset according to which one must avoid the very notion of sin and hence also those of guilt and atonement. Also, by not admitting there is an enemy to fight, one mutes all talk about spiritual struggle. The new pastoral policy imagines a Christianity so pure as to presume itself better and more tolerant than Jesus Christ Himself. Mercy is thus misunderstood in a sentimental way as if it were an irrational passion intended only to alleviate the miseries and sufferings of others.

Indeed, in its sensible aspect, mercy is mere compassion. However, since it is also a rational desire aimed at the good of others, it is a virtue inasmuch as it prudently regulates the movements of the soul. That is why Saint

---

40. John Paul II, *Veritatis splendor*, no. 120.

41. Pius XI, Encyclical *Casti connubii*, Dec. 31, 1930, no. 73, https://w2.vatican.va /content/pius-xi/en/encyclicals/documents/hf_p-xi_enc_19301231_casti -connubii.html.

Paul recommends practicing it reasonably (see Rom. 12:1). Mercy participates affectively in the plight of the poor but only to effectively heal their miseries, beginning with spiritual ones:

> It belongs to mercy to expel defects.[42]

> The Church's way . . . has always been the way of Jesus, the way of mercy and reinstatement. This does not mean underestimating the dangers of letting wolves into the fold, but welcoming the repentant prodigal son; healing the wounds of sin with courage and determination.[43]

Christian mercy is not a way to sweeten and soften life by avoiding problems, struggles, and sacrifices, or evading life's drama. After all, Christianity does not exempt us from the drama of life but prevents it from ending in the tragedy of eternal damnation. Mercy, therefore, presupposes the fear of God: "His mercy is from generation unto generations, to them that fear him" (Luke 1:50), our Lady sings in the Magnificat. Saint Augustine often speaks of the severe mercy with which God, rather than abandoning the sinner to his slumber, shakes him and makes him feel the harsh consequences of his fault, to push him to repentance and conversion.[44]

---

42. St. Thomas, *Summa Theologiae*, I, q. 21, a. 3–4, passim.

43. Pope Francis, "Homily During Mass with the New Cardinals," Feb. 15, 2015, http://w2.vatican.va/content/francesco/en/homilies/2015/documents /papa-francesco_20150215_omelia-nuovi-cardinali.html.

44. See St. Augustine *Confessions*, trans. J.G. Pilkington, in *Nicene and Post-Nicene Fathers*, 1st Series, vol. 1, ed. Philip Schaff (Buffalo, NY: Christian Literature Publishing Co., 1887). Rev. and ed. Kevin Knight for New Advent, http://www.newadvent.org/fathers/1101.htm.

*   *   *

Also, the new pastoral policy presents mercy as if it were completely free. In a sense, this is true, as mercy is not a human right but a Divine gift which does not correspond to merit but far exceeds it. Shakespeare already had Hamlet say: "For God's [sake,] man, much better. Use every man after his desert, and who should escape whipping."[45]

However, this does not mean that mercy has neither rhyme nor reason, much less no purpose. Otherwise, it would not be super-rational and supernatural but irrational and unnatural, that is, false and unjust, unworthy of the God Who does nothing without reason and purpose.

Mercy is free, meaning that it expresses God's sovereign liberty and liberality. However, it emanates from rationality and achieves a higher, supernatural justice, being a gift of the Holy Spirit as rational as the Word from which it emanates.[46]

*   *   *

Furthermore, by the very fact of being free, the new pastoral policy insinuates that mercy should be granted to the sinner without the conditions that show his repentance. If by this the new pastoral policy means that God may grant mercy to a sinner regardless of his prior merits, it is true. If it implies that God does not demand from the sinner the dispositions which He planned and established as necessary for final conversion, then it is false. True mercy leads the sinner to admit his faults and do penance; and if his fault was public, so must be his penance.[47]

---

45. William Shakespeare, *Hamlet*, in *The Complete Works of Shakespeare*, ed. Hardin Craig (Chicago: Scott, Foreman and Co., 1961), act 2, sc. 2, ln. 554.

46. See Antonio Royo Marin, OP, *Teologia de la caridad* (Madrid: B.A.C., 1960), nos. 325–27.

47. See Matt. 18:15–22; *Roman Catechism of the Council of Trent*, nos. 248–62.

> Let the wicked forsake his way, and the un-
> just man his thoughts, and let him return to the
> Lord, and he will have mercy on him, and to our
> God: for he is bountiful to forgive (Isa. 55:7).
>
> Conversion is the most concrete expres-
> sion of the working of love and of the pres-
> ence of mercy in the human world. . . .
>
> Authentic knowledge of the God of mercy,
> the God of tender love, is a constant and in-
> exhaustible source of conversion, not only as
> a momentary interior act but also as a per-
> manent attitude, as a state of mind.[48]

God's fidelity to His promises of salvation demands as
a response mankind's fidelity to its commitment to conversion. But if a sinner invokes divine mercy while refus-
ing to convert, that means he is unwilling to receive that
mercy. "Anyone who deliberately refuses to accept his
mercy by repenting, rejects the forgiveness of his sins and
the salvation offered by the Holy Spirit. Such hardness of
heart can lead to final impenitence and eternal loss."[49]

In this sense, Saint Alphonsus Liguori paradoxically
warned that "the mercy of God sends more souls to hell
than His justice."[50] Therefore, pastors who refrain from
exhorting strayed sheep to conversion should be careful
not to deserve this ancient Divine rebuke: "You . . . have
strengthened the hands of the wicked, that he should
not return from his evil way, and live. Therefore . . . I will

---

48. John Paul II, *Dives in misericordia*, nos. 6, 13.

49. *Catechism of the Catholic Church* (Cita del Vaticano: Libreria Editrice Vaticana,
2003), no. 1864, http://www.vatican.va/archive/ENG0015/_INDEX.HTM.

50. St. Alphonsus Ligouri, *Preparation for Death* (Boston: Thomas Sweeney, 1854),
cons. 23, 2.

deliver my people out of your hand" (Ezech. 13:22–23).

*   *   *

In parallel (and contradicting mercy's gratuity above), the new pastoral policy posits that mercy is due to man by nature. According to this thesis, the human person, being created and redeemed by God in Christ is not only a potential object of divine mercy but is also, necessarily, and unconditionally so, in act. Thus they claim that divine mercy forgives and saves everyone, always, and in any case. If that were so, more than forgiveness, the irrational gratuity of divine mercy would give the sinner a justification for his sins.

However, true mercy is not due in any way to the sinner's human dignity; the prodigal son in the well-known parable is keenly aware of it as "he realizes that he no longer has any right"[51] and humbly asks his father to be welcomed back not as a son but a servant. However, the father sees his son's return home (an image of conversion) as evidence that he has repented for the fault committed: He "was dead and is come to life again" (Luke 15:32). Therefore, the father welcomes his child back home manifesting generous mercy, rather than a mercy that was owed.

In Scripture, God Himself warns there is a time for mercy and forgiveness, but there is also a time for justice and condemnation. Hence, the sinner must take advantage of the time and occasions of mercy that God offers him. Time has a deadline, and opportunities may not return: *"Time Jesum transeuntem et non revententem"* ("Dread the passing of Jesus, for He does not return"), says

---

51. John Paul II, *Dives in misericordia*, no. 5.

an ancient and now forgotten spiritual maxim.

*   *   *

In addition, the new pastoral policy tends to conceive the word mercy as an expression of charity placed in competition to or, alternately, alongside truth. Concern is often shown to warn that truth should not be separated from mercy, which is true: Saint Paul warns that "love, therefore, is the fulfilling of the Law" (Rom. 13:10), "doing truth in charity" (Eph. 4:15). However, sometimes they claim that witnessing to truth is not in itself a merciful action and should be balanced or even externally corrected with mercy; which implies a mercy alien to truth, achieving that very separation they are claiming to avoid.

Indeed, mercy is not a compromise between the demands of truth and those of convenience but rather a balance between rigor and indulgence. Furthermore, by the sheer fact of belonging to the practical field, mercy cannot invade the doctrinal sphere and thus cannot change the moral judgment on a person. Otherwise, such mercy would incur the biblical warning: "Woe to you that call evil good, and good evil: that put darkness for light, and light for darkness: that put bitter for sweet, and sweet for bitter!" (Isa. 5:20).

In short, truth does not need to assume mercy because it is not based on mercy. On the contrary, it is mercy that must presuppose truth, for otherwise, it would not be true mercy. However, truth must be fulfilled in mercy so that it is not realized in the abstract but in real life, from the evangelical perspective of Divine Redemption.

*   *   *

What we have just said about mercy in its relation to

truth can be repeated regarding its relation to justice.

Sometimes, the new pastoral policy seems to conceive mercy as an exception to the right rule or in competition with, or even opposition to, the law.

In reality, mercy does not compete with, let alone oppose, justice. Rather, it is a superior form of justice animated by charity. Mercy tends to supersede just and strict rigor so as to achieve a higher justice, "to restore justice in the sense of that salvific order which God willed from the beginning in man,"[52] so that mercy and justice will kiss (see Ps. 84:11).

> What is compassion but a fellow-feeling for another's misery, which prompts us to help him if we can? And this emotion is obedient to reason, when compassion is shown without violating right.[53]

> There is much wanting both to discipline and to compassion, if one be had without the other.[54]

> God acts mercifully, not indeed by going against His justice, but by doing something more than justice. . . . Hence it is clear that mercy does not destroy justice, but in a sense is the fullness thereof. And thus it is said: 'Mercy exalteth itself above judgment' (James 2:13).[55]

> Such a generous requirement of forgiveness

---

52. John Paul II, *Dives in misericordia*, no. 7.

53. St. Augustine, *City of God*, bk. 9, ch. 5.

54. St. Gregory, *Pastoral Care*, bk. 2, ch. 6.

55. St. Thomas, *Summa Theologicae*, I, q. 21, a. 3.

> does not cancel out the objective requirements
> of justice.... In any case, reparation for evil and
> scandal, compensation for injury, and satisfac-
> tion for insult are conditions for forgiveness.[56]
>
> What is unacceptable is the attitude of one
> who makes his own weakness the criterion
> of the truth about the good, so that he can
> feel self-justified.... An attitude of this sort
> corrupts the morality of society as a whole,
> since it encourages doubt about the objectiv-
> ity of the moral law.[57]

As a result, true mercy does not exclude punishing the sinner but presupposes it because it has an atoning power that can convert and heal the culprit.[58] "A Jesus who agrees with everything and everyone, a Jesus without his holy wrath, without the harshness of truth and true love is not the real Jesus as the Scripture shows but a miserable caricature. A conception of 'gospel' in which the seriousness of God's wrath is absent has nothing to do with the biblical Gospel."[59]

*   *   *

The new pastoral policy sometimes seems even to claim that mercy involves putting oneself in the shoes of the poor, the weak, and the servants, as it would be the only way to show solidarity with them. Some infer that the Church should become poor, weak and a servant and refrain from proposing overly arduous goals to the modern faithful and retreating to expectations that are

---

56. John Paul II, *Dives in misericordia*, no. 14.

57. John Paul II, *Veritatis splendor*, no. 104.

58. See Matt. 25:31–46; St. Thomas, *Summa Theologicae*, II–IIae, q. 19, a. 1.

59. Joseph Ratzinger, *Guardare a Cristo* (Milan: Jaca Book, 1986), 76.

proportional to man, i.e. to today's weak humanity.

Also, we often hear that holiness today is a journey too arduous to sustain so the pastor should limit himself to place the flock on merciful paths that lead to a so-called lesser evil to thus supposedly reduce the harm. Therefore, in the pharmacopeia proposed by the new pastoral policy, mercy is served up as a pleasing mash to replace the overly dense and bitter medicine of justice.

In truth, "God has not given us the spirit of fear, but of power" (2 Tim. 1:7) which pushes us to desire the highest goods and to practice the most difficult virtues, "doing slave labor, but with the spirit of a hero."[60]

Therefore, the Church has the mission to treat and heal sinners like the Good Samaritan who rescued the unfortunate victim of his own recklessness who took a dangerous route threatened by the Enemy (see Luke 10:30–37). But in so doing, a prudent Samaritan can neither underrate the situation of the victim nor mislead him about the security of the road traveled. Instead, he must remain lucid to warn the patient about the severity of his state and teach him how to avoid enemy ambushes.

As a matter of fact, if we fail to teach him the ideal goals, today's man will never have a reason to convert and strive for perfection but will remain satisfied with his misery. This severely impairs his possibilities of healing.

---

60. Joseph Huby, SJ, *San Paolo: Epistole della prigionia* (Rome: Studium, 1960), 264.

CHAPTER 3
Listening
A Premise of the New Pastoral Policy

According to current theology, a pastoral policy animated by mercy must first respectfully *listen* to the flock, and especially to sheep in difficult situations.

What Does *Listening* Mean?

By definition, listening means to hear someone attentively. In this sense, the pastor has a duty to bend over his sheep to listen to them, so as to evaluate their state of tranquility or disquiet, health, or disease. From the religious standpoint, listening to the faithful only makes sense when it allows us to understand what aspects can lead them to conversion or hinder it, thus facilitating conversion through the removal of obstacles.

What Is Meant now by Listening?

In the new pastoral policy, however, listening is understood in a talismanic way. Indeed, in this context, listening is not a passive "hearing" but an active "coming out of oneself" to meet the other party, stoop to his level, "look with his eyes," "beat with his heart," identify with him and "share his situation." This assumes that the listener be free from prejudices and inhibiting conventions.

Therefore, the shepherd must not so much watch over his flock but place himself in harmony and identify with them. Every single sheep has a right to be respectfully understood, for otherwise it will feel neglected or even despised and in danger of leaving the flock. After all—the new pastoral policy says—what good is freedom of speech in the Church if it does not include a right of the faithful to be heard by their superiors?

Listening presupposes respecting the speaker's authenticity which, as we have seen, now vicariously replaces a rightly formed conscience. For the listening pastoral policy, it is no longer important for man to be in harmony with the Divine will, but only to be sincere and at peace with himself and others. His harmony and peace with God follows automatically.

In a further step, a pastoral policy of listening requires the Church to restrict herself to hearing the questions posed by the faithful, without providing solutions. In this perspective, the Church, which once was above all a Teacher, that is, she taught, today tends to become a Church that mostly *listen*s, *dialogues*, and *questions* herself without fearing to cast into doubt indisputable certainties and essential assurances.

However, such listening reduces the ecclesiastical hierarchy to the condition of a teacher who can teach only what his pupils ask to learn. In this way, the magisterial function of the Church ends up being subject to the approval of the faithful, or rather of the lobbies capable of mobilizing them. Moreover, in the context of this listening, the bleating of repentant sheep and those who strive to observe the Commandments are often muffled by that of impenitent sheep who seek to legitimize their immoral life.

Primacy of Listening Over Teaching

This pastoral policy approach has launched a new slogan: The *primacy of listening* over ecclesiastical prerogatives, above all over teaching but also over judging, admonishing, and correcting. The pastor should no longer check the sincerity and above all honesty of his sheep, but merely ascertain that their opinions and decisions are authentic. At most he can respectfully disagree with them, but cannot pretend to impose anything.

The primacy of listening requires a certain precedence and preeminence of the base over authority in the management of the Church. For example, pastors are required to carry out sociological surveys (questionnaires, polls, and statistics) not only to learn about the concrete situation of the flock, but also to decide what is to be done in its favor. The fact that the Holy See asked ecclesial grassroots (institutions, associations, movements, communities, families) to make proposals to the 2015 Synod that could not be ignored gave the impression of being influenced by sociological data.

However, as is well known, sociological surveys can raise serious reservations as to their methods. For example, questions can be formulated in a tendentious way so as to suggest a particular answer. Consequently, responses may distort reality by favoring some issues over others, for example, the marginal over the central, the emotional over the doctrinal, and the pathological over the normal. In essence, the family image distilled from the answers seems to resemble more that which is propagated by the secularist culture, through the mass media, than reality.[61]

Therefore, such primacy of listening over teaching may instill relativism into the ecclesial mentality and sensitivity. The Church's mission is not so much to listen and talk to men but to convert and sanctify them.

---

61. See Pagotto et al., *Preferential Option*.

Once listening has prevailed over teaching, Church Magisterium and government are likely to be reduced to the ascertaining and execution of the grassroots' requests: The *Ecclesia docens* (Teaching Church) will depend on the *Ecclesia discens* (Learning Church). Were that to happen the Church would be structured as an inverted pyramid.

CHAPTER 4

Discernment

Method to Diagnose Pastoral Situations

According to current theology, a pastoral policy that is animated by mercy and listens to the flock must exercise a *discernment* that can diagnose situations experienced by the sheep.

What Is the Meaning of Discernment?

By definition, discernment is the ability to make a judgment or choose a behavior according to the requirements of a situation. This allows one to judge persons and events so as to unite what should be united and divide what should be divided.

Discernment requires not only knowledge of a person in his particular situation but also, and especially, in reference to an upright criterion of judgment and an objective standard of assessment aiming to achieve the *justum*, i.e. an ethical truth. On the other hand, this requires distinguishing between various persons and situations that have to be judged differently, a perception that is often criticized now as *discrimination*.

One cannot discern without judging. The famous evangelical prohibition of judgment (see Luke 6:37) only affects rash judgment, which often proves to be wrong and unfair because it seeks to scrutinize a person's inner conscience.[62] Here, it is not a question of judging

---

62. [Ed.: See St. Thomas, *Summa Theologiae*, II-II, q. 60, a. 2.]

consciences, but ideas and actions.

What Is Meant now by Discernment?

As we have seen, new theology postulates the primacy of pastoral policy over doctrine, of conscience over the Law, of listening over teaching. Accordingly, to comply with this primacy the new pastoral policy employs discernment as a diagnostic method to analyze problematic situations, such as family and social ones.

The new pastoral policy implies that one should always assume man's fundamental goodness and good faith, even against all evidence, so as to recognize the absolute dignity of the human person, which deserves an equally absolute confidence.

In this perspective, discernment avoids examining a person or situation in the light of truth and the law, so as to judge him abstractly from the outside, comparing him to an extraneous model, seeking to lead him back to the moral and ecclesial order. Rather, discernment undertakes to examine the person or situation from within the light of his conscience, considering the person in his demands, so as to evaluate him in his living authenticity.

This method—the new pastoral policy claims—allows for the saving of what remains valid and sincere in people and situations. Accordingly, they should not be judged by their actions but by their intent. They should not be judged for the evil done or unrepaired but for the residual or potential good still within them. However, by evaluating according to subjective and situational criteria, this pastoral discernment risks confusing the fake with the sincere, the emotional with the rational, the exception with the rule, and, in practice, allowing all behavior, however unjustified in theory.

This pastoral policy approach gives rise to talismanic maxims and slogans of some importance and success. Let us see a few.

Primacy of Discernment Over Judgment

The primacy of listening over teaching translates into a parallel and consequent *primacy of discernment over judgment* which warns against judging and poses the rhetorical question: "Who am I to judge?"

Thus, in a first stage, the method of pastoral evaluation is one that avoids judging or, if compelled to do so, tries to judge *mercifully,* without condemning or punishing. Indeed, the assumption is that the sinner should be pitied as the victim of an untenable situation, or, better, an oppressive society. What matters is not to judge a person's guilt or innocence, but only to assess his situation and encourage rehabilitation.

In a second stage, pastoral discernment paradoxically leads to the forbidding of any condemning judgment that would be seen as pretending to evaluate a person from outside himself, according to his supposed conformity to a moralistic model. Instead, discernment assesses the person from within, taking into account his pastoral situations, intentions, and possibilities.

If strictly implemented, in a third stage, discernment switches from absolving the transgressor of the law to condemning courts that apply the law, institutions that enshrine it, and even the law itself, as being too demanding for our age. The result is the end of legal certainty, impunity, and general anarchy.

Note that this methodological approach is influenced by recent, permissive theories on criminal law which, obsessed with avoiding unjust or excessive sentences, end up questioning, on the one hand, the offender's responsibility, and, on the other, the whole judicial institution. Were this to happen, it would become impossible not only for a court to issue a ruling, but even to formulate an upright judgment.

Respect for the Other or Different

Among the words of talismanic value that are dominant in current ecclesial language, the adjectives *other* and *different* are worth mentioning.

According to the new pastoral policy, discernment presupposes not just the listening to, but also the *respect for the other or different*. Not surprisingly, the term other is used mostly as an indefinite pronoun, for by its very lack of definition it may signify not only that which is partially or entirely different from something, but indeed that which is its exact opposite. Hence, respect for the other requires also respecting that which is the opposite of what is considered to be true, good, and right.

From this perspective, the person who denies truth, refuses goodness, and violates justice is not a sinner, but one who does not agree with an established authority (family, civil society, institutions, State, Church). In short, he is only one who thinks and acts differently, one who follows other rules.

Thus, we should avoid harassing this different person with reproaches, condemnations, and punishments. Instead, we must respectfully listen to him, as much as possible, and we should especially value his diversity, even if it questions political, family, moral, and even religious certainties—as happens with irregular and same-sex couples, for example.

As can be seen, this discernment—which goes so far

as to admit only that which is different, by giving it a right of citizenship and power in society and the Church—is another factor likely to instill relativism and permissiveness. For example, the new pastoral policy speaks now of a "different sexuality," a "different parenting" and "diverse families" in referring to those who violate sexual and family morality.

This stems from the fact that in contemporary culture the words other and different have become the subject of widespread and incessant propaganda that has broadened and distorted their meaning. Inside the Church, these two terms have been submitted to a bewildering exegesis that has turned them sacred, as it were, to the point of idolatry. Suffice it to recall that certain theological language elevates the categories of otherness and diversity to icons, as God is seen as "wholly other," and Jesus is understood as the model of a discriminated and marginalized offender. Here we have a typical case in which the politically correct is not just achieved, but surpassed by the religiously correct.

Complex Situations

Having become aware of the diversity of people and circumstances, the new pastoral policy seeks to apply special discernment above all to those who find themselves in *complex situations.*

By definition, the adjective complex means resulting from the union of different parts or interdependent elements, indicating a reality difficult to understand or classify.

However, in the new ecclesiastical language complex situations simply mean irregular or immoral ones whose problematic nature requires circumstantial diagnosis and therapy. Cohabiting or divorce-remarried couples are well-known examples of this.

The linguistic deception lies in defining a situation with a euphemistic adjective (complex) that cloaks its original illicit or immoral aspect, which would allow an ethical evaluation. It is well known that people resort to euphemism and circumlocutions when afraid of calling something by its name. In our case, the conclusion is that this situation cannot be clearly judged or resolved. And so, complexity becomes an excuse to evade the issue and prevent its decisive but unpleasant cure.

Hurt Persons, Couples, and Families

So-called *hurt couples* and *hurt families* stand out among the different when it comes to marriage and family life. The new pastoral policy especially listens to and applies discernment in assessing their complex situations.

In truth, any therapy should carefully distinguish between two very different kinds of wounds.[63] There are those who have been hurt by others and thus innocently suffer the consequences of the sin of others, for example, people who have been betrayed or abandoned by their spouse, or children who have been abandoned by their parents. But there are also those who have injured themselves and so culpably suffer the consequences of their sin, for example, those who have left their spouse or children. These two species are different, have different responsibilities, and, therefore, should be treated differently. The hurt *innocent* should be especially encouraged to have patience and forgiveness, while the injured *culprits*

---

63. [Ed. Catholic progressives see sin not as an offense against God, but merely a wound in the person. They focus only on its emotive or circumstantial repercussion in a person and are silent about its essence: how it offends God who has the right to be obeyed.]

must first be exhorted to repent, to do penance, and to repair the harm done. The attention and mercy deserved by the former are very different from those that may be shown the latter.

In the current ecclesial and media debate the hurt person expression alludes especially to those who suffer the painful consequences of an immoral situation because they live in a state of habitual, serious, and public sin: adultery, partnership, concubinage, divorced-remarried, homosexual couples, and so forth.

Until recently they were just referred to as public sinners, but according to the new pastoral policy, that was a merciless and outdated moral condemnation that would risk irritating further those sensitive persons. Today, by euphemistically calling them hurt persons one avoids expressing a preventive moral condemnation by emphasizing a single, true, but secondary aspect: their concrete situation. This term lends itself to stimulating compassion: "They are just hurt, perhaps innocent victims!"[64]

In a first stage, the talismanic word merely exploits understandable compassion. The normal reaction when faced with a hurt person is to come closer, to give him comfort and help. In our case, in order not to exacerbate the psychological suffering of the irregular person (or couple, or family), any moral judgment about him is discouraged, being considered offensive and harmful. Instead, a merciful attitude of solidarity with him is recommended as the only acceptable one to implement effective pastoral policy.

In a second stage, the compassionate feeling triggers a progressive identification with the hurt person that

---

64. See Pagotto et al., *Preferential Option*, ch. 11.

makes us forget his responsibility. In order not to make
him feel guilty and reconcile him with himself and the
Church, the initial suspension of moral judgment becomes reversed: His situation is now excused or even
justified as insurmountable, while those who persist in
admonishing him are accused of lacking mercy.

If what the new pastoral policy advocates were
true, then the famous and magnificent parable of the
Good Samaritan would need to be updated to today's
mentality. Paradoxically, this is how it would end: In
his effort to spare the wounded man further suffering,
the Samaritan minimizes the seriousness of his
wounds and does not apply the painful remedies that
might heal him. Thus, the Samaritan merely adminis-
ters palliatives which, though alleviating pain, end up
ensuring the victim's permanence in his unfortunate
state while rendering him oblivious to his condition.
Naturally, to avoid disturbing the victim with bad feel-
ings the Samaritan refrains from warning him to avoid
the dangerous road on which he was attacked, so the
poor man risks being mugged once again. The moral
of this revised and corrected parable: You would be
much better off trying to heal on your own than to be
helped by a Samaritan like this!

Imperfect Couples and Families

Pastoral discernment requires that hurt couples or families no longer be criticized as immoral or irregular but
only referred to as *imperfect.*

By definition, imperfect means partially unfinished, deficient, and, therefore, defective. But there are different
types of imperfections: Some are light and excusable as
they do not harm the integrity of the subject (such as a

family) while others are serious and inexcusable because they harm it unto ruin.

Trusting in sociological surveys and mass-media propaganda, the new pastoral policy is inclined to believe that it is now extremely hard to find couples or families who are perfect in every aspect. Therefore, a healthy realism demands that one resign oneself to the growing prevalence of imperfect couples and families, with whom society and also the Church must continue to live.

Here, too, the euphemistic change of adjective (from immoral to irregular, and then to imperfect) favors a change not only of sensitivity and style but also in the moral evaluation, usually in a permissive and tendentiously exculpatory sense. On the other hand, given that nothing in the world is really perfect, who would dare condemn someone for the sole reason of being incomplete, deficient, or defective in something?

Now then, obviously no couple or family is perfect in everything like the exemplary Holy Family of Nazareth was. This notwithstanding, a couple living in the scandalous state of concubinage cannot be characterized as merely imperfect, but must be judged to be immoral, since they are public sinners. In classifying them as an imperfect couple and pitying them as victims, one not only violates truth and justice, but also wrongs the couple itself, who will feel, if not justified in their sin, at least as bearing diminished responsibility for it, thus running the risk of ending up confirmed in their evil state.

At the end of the process, irregular couples or families will not only be excused, but also accepted as they are, in other words, justified in their immorality, with severe damage to the moral sense, and to the common good of society and the Church. Thus, one will come to tolerate evil and accept it as normal.

The gap between the new and the classical pastoral policy can be measured by this warning from a Pope who was not known for his severity: "Rather than employ sweet and temporizing words, a parish priest should sternly exhort cohabiters not to commit such a grave crime and not to sin against the Divine Law."[65]

---

65. Pius VII, Brief *Etsi fraternitatis*, Aug. 10, 1803.

CHAPTER 5

Accompaniment

The New Pastoral Policy's Therapeutic Method

In the new pastoral policy, listening to and practicing discernment of the faithful that are hurt and in complex situations requires shepherds to show care for them, by *accompanying* them along their journey.

What Does *Accompaniment* Mean?

By definition, to accompany means to follow someone, to keep him company, or protect him. In the Christian perspective, the only valid accompaniment is one that leads man to God along the way of salvation, which is Jesus Christ.[66] Therefore, the shepherd must guide the flock by making it "walk worthy of the vocation in which you are called" (Eph. 4:1), in other words, in a saintly way. The pastor should bring about the conversion of sheep gone astray in the sense of their making an about face, to return to the path leading to the Sheepfold. However, if a sheep gives scandal and refuses to convert, it must be isolated and banished from the fold, as Saint Paul teaches: "But now I have written to you, not to keep company, if any man that is named a brother, be a fornicator, or covetous, or a server of idols, or a railer, or a drunkard, or an extortioner: with such a one, not so much as to eat. . . . Put away

---

66. See Pope Francis, Apostolic Exhortation *Evangelii Gaudium*, Nov. 24, 2013, no. 179, http://w2.vatican.va/content/francesco/en/apost_exhortations /documents/papa-francesco_esortazione-ap_20131124_evangelii-gaudium.html.

the evil one from among yourselves" (1 Cor. 5:11–13).

What Is Understood by Accompaniment Today?

The new pastoral policy implies accompaniment in a very different way, raising it to a therapeutic method: For weak souls, keeping them company is seen as the best comfort and solidarity as the best medicine.

In a first stage of accompaniment one just needs to follow the person along his life pilgrimage, moving with him through the stages of his adventure. This assumes that the pastor not lead the flock, as its guide, but rather follow them, as a fellow traveler.

In a second stage, having grown accustomed to following his faithful, the shepherd stops questioning the righteousness of the path his flock takes and no longer tries to change its course, but at most, to change its speed. Accordingly, the duty of solidarity prevails over the right to judge and command. It is thus insinuated that the Church has no right to teach a pilgrim the way to go, nor seek to force him to follow it, but should limit herself to discovering the right way with him, and then follow him, sharing his fate.

According to this view, we should not be overly worried if the faithful have taken a wrong path. The important thing is not to treat them as if they were minors that need protection, let alone wayward souls or lost sheep to be corrected, as was once the case. In fact, we must avoid imposing a predetermined destination on them claiming to know the paths established by God. To paraphrase an old slogan, one could say that, "the goal is nothing, the way is everything," so that, however dangerous, every way leads to salvation, provided man freely chooses it.

On the other hand, the new theology posits that Divine condescension always accompanies the human journey without questioning it, no matter where it leads. In fact, it is often said that today "man is the way of the Church" in the sense that the only path She should follow is the one taken by humanity in its history. But this implies that man should follow not so much Jesus Christ but their own destiny. Their goal is no longer eternity but the "omega point" of the cosmic-historical evolution.[67] In short, *sequela Christi* [following Christ] is replaced by *sequela Hominis*.

At the end of the process, one risks forgetting the Gospel teaching that Jesus Christ is man's only Way, Truth, Justice and eternal salvation; that eternal life is the only goal one must pursue; and that pastors have the duty to bring strayed sheep back into the Fold.

Accompaniment of Cultural and Social Processes

Having established that man must be accompanied, by following him along the stages of his life without trying to convert him through proselytizing, the new pastoral policy stipulates that human society must also be accompanied and followed in its historical evolution without trying to convert it by imposing a Christian model. All that matters is that, like man, society too follow its conscience, by consistently moving along the way it has freely chosen in striving for universal brotherhood.

---

67. [Ed.—This is a reference to the mystic-pantheistic theories of Fr. Teilhard de Chardin regarding which, in 1962, the Sacred Congregation for the Holy Office issued a *monitum*, a "Warning Regarding the Writings of Father Teilhard de Chardin," confirmed by the Communiqué of the Press Office of the Holy See (*L'Osservatore Romano*, Jul. 20, 1981, English edition), https://www.ewtn.com /library/CURIA/CDFTEILH.HTM.]

Therefore, the Church should limit itself to become society's fellow traveler to serve it, not in the abstract, but in its concrete, historical, and social evolution. The task of the ecclesiastical hierarchy is solely to follow society by providing a spiritual supplement of soul to help it fulfill its destiny.

This approach also applies to the social institution of the family: The Church must accompany its cultural processes, follow its historical evolution, and encourage its modernization in a pluralistic sense, without seeking to impose a historically obsolete model (e.g. patriarchal, paternalistic, bourgeois).

However, one must object that current cultural and social processes are neither neutral nor tend toward rational or natural models, let alone Christian ones, but rather foster subversive ways of life and types of behavior, and seek to impose them on society, banning all forms of dissent and resistance. To accompany these processes implies following them, experiencing them, engaging in them, and finally approving and adapting to them. Ultimately, this means not only giving up Christian civilization but also helping to build an anti-Christian civilization.

By contrast, a responsible and merciful shepherd cannot allow his sheep to venture outside the Fold and stray onto paths that end in ravines. Nor can pastoral policy encourage the faithful to render themselves accomplices of processes that take them toward ruin.

Pastoral Policy of *Closeness*

If you want to accompany someone, first you need to stay close to him. Thus, the therapeutic method of accompaniment assumes the *pastoral policy of closeness* summed up in the slogan, "to draw closer."

This approach requires that the shepherd draw close to every potential sheep and not exclude or banish any. As a consequence, for the Church, no one is far away or a stranger, let alone an enemy. The only ones still distant are those to whom we have not yet drawn closer, due to our prejudice against the different.

The new pastoral policy of closeness is reduced to a process that aims to achieve harmony and osmosis with one's neighbor by putting oneself in his shoes and accepting him as he as is. We must have an existential experience of our neighbor, to serve him by allowing ourselves to be engaged by him, and by sharing desires and projects. Thus, we need to establish not only a relationship of closeness but also one of cultural and moral adaptation.

By contrast, a truly charitable and merciful pastoral policy of closeness should favor an honest apostolate that aims to lead our neighbor closer to truth and justice. When dealing with people who live in error or sin, outside the Church or on its margins, we should admonish them, offering the bitter but healing medicine of reproach. To his strayed sheep, a pastor must repeat God's admonition to Cain: "If you act rightly, you will be accepted; but if not, sin lies in wait at the door: its urge is for you, yet *you can rule over it*" (Gen. 4:7–NABRE). You can save your soul by converting and overcoming the inclination to sin.

And if it comes to public scandal, "Them that sin reprove before all: that the rest also may have fear" (1 Tim. 5:20). "The bishop must not ignore the sinner but must rebuke him so that others may turn cautious."[68]

---

68. *Didache—The Lord's Teaching Through the Twelve Apostles to the Nations*, trans. M.B. Riddle, in *Ante-Nicene Fathers*, vol. 7, ed. by Alexander Roberts, et. al. (Buffalo, NY: Christian Literature Publishing Co., 1886), 17. Rev. and ed. Kevin Knight for New Advent, http://www.newadvent.org/fathers/0714.htm.

God Himself warns: "Such as I love, I rebuke and chastise" (Apoc. 3:19) for "reproofs of instruction are the way of life" (Prov. 6:23).

And Saint Augustine warns: "Do not imagine that you... then love your neighbor when you do not rebuke him: this is not charity, but mere feebleness. Let charity be fervent to correct, to amend."[69]

> Consider what the things are that [your enemy] takes from you: not even them would he take from you, but by permission of Him who "scourges every son whom He receives" (Heb. 12:6.) He, this same enemy of yours, is in a manner the instrument in the hands of God, by which you may be healed. If God knows it to be good for you that he should despoil you, He permits him; if He knows it to be good for you that you should receive blows, He permits him to smite you: by the means of Him He cares for you: wish that he may be made whole.[70]

Therefore,

> The ruler should be, through humility, a companion of good livers, and, through the zeal of righteousness, rigid against the vices of evil-doers. . . . But there ought to be in rulers towards their subjects both compassion justly

69. St. Augustine, Homily 7 on the First Epistle of John, trans. H. Browne, in Nicene and Post-Nicene Fathers, 1st Series, Vol. 7, ed. Philip Schaff (Buffalo, NY: Christian Literature Publishing Co., 1888), 11. Rev. and ed. Kevin Knight for New Advent, http://www.newadvent.org/fathers/170207.htm.

70. St. Augustine, Homily 8 on the First Epistle of John, trans. H. Browne, in Nicene and Post-Nicene Fathers, 1st Series, Vol. 7, ed. Philip Schaff (Buffalo, NY: Christian Literature Publishing Co., 1888), 11. Rev. and ed. Kevin Knight for New Advent, http://www.newadvent.org/fathers/170208.htm.

considerate, and discipline affectionately severe. . . . Gentleness, then, is to be mingled with
severity; a sort of compound is to be made of
both; so that subjects be neither [exasperated]
by too much asperity, nor relaxed by too great
kindness. . . . Wherefore let there be love, but
not enervating; let there be vigor, but not ex-
asperating; let there be zeal, but not immod-
erately burning; let there be pity; but not
sparing more than is expedient; that, while
justice and mercy blend themselves together
in supreme rule, he who is at the head may
both soothe the hearts of his subjects in making them afraid, and yet in soothing them con-
strain them to reverential awe.[71]

The Church as a *Field Hospital*

The two Synods on the family have raised the striking
image of a Church conceived as a field hospital that
should receive and treat all those hurt through misfortune or even by their transgressions.

Since Jesus Christ is the Divine Doctor, it is certainly
true that His Church should be organized as a hospital
able to treat and cure the wounded, minding however
that the really dangerous evils are solely those that affect
the soul not the body, as they do not send man to physical
death, which comes in any case, but to spiritual demise.
Today it is said that the Church must gear up in the manner of a field hospital built to remedy the consequences
of an ongoing spiritual war.

Now then, that being the case the new pastoral policy
should first of all explain what that war is about, how
and when it started, who is the enemy that declared it,

---

71. St. Gregory, *Pastoral Care*, bk. 2, ch. 6

on what ground the fighting takes place, what are the weapons used, what wounds they cause, what diseases they spread, what therapies should be employed to cure them, what medication to use, in short, how we can defeat the enemy and win the war. Above all, the new pastoral policy should explain how the much-vaunted modernity has caused this war that requires a field hospital. Instead, with the new pastoral policy everything risks remaining without explanation, strategies, or proposed solutions, other than welcoming the needy, caring for the wounded, and working for peace: An obvious but vague proposal, since it applies to any situation.

Moreover, this highly dramatic scenario contrasts with the optimistic, sentimental, and feel-good climate spread by the talismanic words and magic slogans we are examining. They do not lead to a general mobilization but rather to smiling demobilization. If the current situation of the Church is similar to that of an order of military chaplains who must play good Samaritans to win the war and solve problems, what is needed is not the good will of a group of amateur nurses to assuage the pain of the wounded by administering palliatives that only render their ills chronic or applying poultices that cause their sores to rot. Long ago, a great prophet lamented: "They have treated lightly the injury to my people: 'Peace, peace!' they say, though there is no peace" (Jer. 6:14).

Instead, there is a need for competent intervention by medical surgeons who, at the cost of being importunate to the wounded, bravely save them from death by amputating their diseased parts. Only then can the patients heal and bless the doctors who saved them. Saint Augustine proposes subjecting sick people to this healing care:

> [The surgeon's knife] takes away the rotten-
> ness, and seems to make the wound greater.
> Behold, when the rottenness was in the body,
> the wound was less, but perilous: then comes
> the knife; the wound smarted less than
> it smarts now while the [surgeon] is cutting it.
> It smarts more while he is operating upon it
> than it would if it were not operated upon;
> it smarts more under the healing operation,
> but only that it may never smart when the
> healing is effected. Then let fear occupy your
> heart, that it may bring in charity; let the [scar]
> succeed to the [surgeon's] knife. He is such
> an Healer, that the [scars] do not even appear:
> only put yourself under His hand. For if you be
> without fear, you cannot be justified.[72]

Partial Communion With God and the Church

The new pastoral policy tends to justify applying discernment and accompaniment to those in complex situations
on the grounds they are still in partial or imperfect communion with God and the Church and thus cannot be re-
fused any Sacrament, even those reserved for persons in
the state of grace, such as the Holy Eucharist.

Sometimes pastoral openness presupposes, at least
implicitly, a doctrinal novelty. In our case, it is introduced
by two principles: The so-called law of gradualness, according to which one can admit a partial conformity to
Christian morality; and the gradualness of communion,
according to which one can admit a partial union with
the Church and with God Himself.

---

72. St. Augustine, *Homily 9 on the First Epistle of John*, trans. by H. Browne, in *Nicene and Post-Nicene Fathers*, 1st Series, Vol. 7, ed. by Philip Schaff (Buffalo, NY: Christian Litera-ture Publishing Co., 1888), 4. Rev. and ed. Kevin Knight for New Advent, http://www.newadvent.org/fathers/170209.htm.

Everything starts from the premise that it is unrealistic to expect a sinner to convert by subjecting himself to decisions or renunciations imposed by the logic of "all at once and entirely" or "all or nothing." Consequently, people and couples in irregular situations need to be accompanied applying the law of gradualness, that is, by discerning their degree of involvement in the situation they experience and their level of awareness of the moral and religious law they violated. If the sinner's involvement and awareness are partial, so is his responsibility. Hence, he is only partially guilty for the situation in which he lives.

Therefore, the new pastoral policy hopes that the Christian community will deal indulgently with these sinners, appreciate the positive values they retain, and avoid criticizing their remaining shortcomings. Thus, they cannot be relegated to the margins of the Church, but must be allowed to participate, at least partially, in ecclesial and sacramental life.

Consequently, in the new pastoral policy, compliance with canon law and Gospel morality, communion with the Church and even union with God can be partial, according to a scale of values with higher or lesser degrees, but all of them valid. Between someone living in mortal sin and one living in the state of grace, between those who deny God and those who are united to Him, there are only different degrees of perfection; not a qualitative, but only a quantitative difference.

That being the case, no one can be considered to be outside the Church, for the simple fact—the new pastoral policy claims—that God has united himself to every man at least in a way, to some degree. Hence, all men are partially believers and in the state of grace.

However, this also means that all are partially unbelievers and in the state of sin.

For example, the new pastoral policy tends to argue that those in immoral situations might be in partial compliance with the evangelical law and in partial communion with the Church. This insinuates that the Church could now admit divorce, concubinage, remarriage, and (also homosexual) cohabitation for hurt people and couples convinced of finding themselves in irremediable situations, unable to maintain or recover a true marriage commitment.

That begs the question: How can a Christian be a partial believer, partially in the state of grace, or partially married? How can a man be *"simul justus et peccator,"* as Luther advocated? How can the Church restrict herself to accompanying someone and attest to his partial holiness and impiety without trying to convert him? Does this not end up perhaps in relativizing morality and Faith, and in justifying sin?

This approach is so incoherent that the *sensus fidei* requires us to raise this objection: Gradual awareness of the Law and progressive compliance with it, do not allow man to dwell in partial adherence to morality. For example, a person that seriously violates even one Commandment out of ten cannot be pleasing to God, even partially: "And whosoever shall keep the whole law, but offend in one point, is become guilty of all" (James 2:10). Thus the famous principle of Dionysius Areopagite, taken up by Saint Augustine and Saint Thomas, remains valid: *"bonum ex integra causa, malum ex quocumque defectu"* (an action is good when good in every respect; it is wrong when wrong in any respect).

In fact, the one instance presented as an application

of the law of gradualness is rather a case of the gradualness of the law condemned by John Paul II:

> [Married people] cannot however look on the law as *merely an ideal* to be achieved in the future: they must consider it as a command of Christ the Lord to overcome difficulties with constancy. "And so what is known as 'the law of gradualness' or step-by-step advance cannot be identified with 'gradualness of the law,' as if there were *different degrees or forms* of precept in God's law for different individuals and situations. . . ." [John Paul II, Homily at the Close of the Sixth Synod of Bishops (Oct. 25, 1980)].[73]

---

73. John Paul II, *Familiaris consortio*, no. 34. (Our emphasis.)

CHAPTER 6

Integration
The New Pastoral Policy's Ultimate Goal

The new pastoral policy argues that welcoming must be accomplished by fully and unconditionally *integrating* into society and the Church those who have so far been excluded or marginalized to existential peripheries for being deemed different.

What Does *Integration* Mean?

By definition, integration means incorporation by excluding all discrimination. In short, to integrate means to insert something into a whole so that it becomes an organic part of it.

Note that two conditions are necessary to integrate something or someone into an integral whole. First, the integrating whole must be able to assimilate the elements it welcomes organically; second, those elements must be susceptible to assimilation by the whole so as to become an integral part thereof and be rid of any lingering foreign elements that may cause rejection, as in organ transplants. While biological and medical examples that illustrate this rule are many, we leave them to the reader as here we are interested in those regarding integration into the body of society and that of the Church.

For a Christian, to be integrated into the Church involves believing in the truths She transmits, obeying her laws, receiving her sacraments, and being guided by her legitimate shepherds. Those outside the Church can only be integrated through a conversion that requires abjuring their errors and repenting for their sins.[74]

What Is Meant now by Integration?

In the context of the new pastoral policy, this word too risks taking on a talismanic and misleading meaning. The integration desired now is merely insertion, as it does not require assimilation of the parts by the whole. There are plans to insert into society or the Church elements that are not susceptible of being assimilated as they remain foreign to them. In this way, the organic whole not only fails to integrate them but, with their inclusion, risks disintegrating. In short, what is being sought is a paradoxical disintegrating integration.

Take the example of irregular persons, couples, or families. The slogan is: "They should be welcomed and integrated into the Church hospital first, and then eventually healed." Hence, the new pastoral policy plans to insert them into the Church as they are, without public repentance or reparation. Only after that integration, and because of it, can one try to rectify their irregularities.

However, it is one thing to cure the spiritually sick outside the Church mercifully, and another to seek to fully integrate them into the ecclesial body at the risk of infecting the healthy. Only those who are fully converted or at least well on their way to conversion, having demonstrated this by leaving the state of public sin (for example, by abandoning what was once called concubinage) and by following a penitential path similar to those once employed, can be accepted or reintegrated into the Church.

---

74. See *Catechism of the Catholic Church*, nos. 815, 837.

Unrepentant public sinners cannot be readmitted to the life of the Church as they are. If that were to happen, as foreign elements they would not only fail to integrate into the community but would disintegrate it, inevitably and understandably causing scandal and rejection by the still healthy parts of the ecclesial body.

This utopian thesis of unconditional integration has been launched by multiple slogans formulated as categorical imperatives. Let us see a few.

"Embrace Diversity"

By definition, *welcoming* means willingness to receive a stranger into a group; the act of making a guest feel at home by finding that his presence is welcome.

Strictly speaking, the obligation to integrate anyone assumes that every person has an absolute value and therefore must be accepted as is, without having to convert. Of course, this also applies to irregular persons, couples, and families, as we have already seen.

In a first stage, the word welcoming is understood in the egalitarian sense of receiving anyone, any which way, and anywhere, so that no one feels excluded, and without weighing the possible consequences that will have in the social or ecclesial body.

In a second stage, from egalitarian, the welcoming turns selective, by adopting a preferential option for the different, supposedly in greater need or more deserving than others.

At the end of this process, the selective welcoming becomes discriminating by excluding those who do not accept this pastoral method, for in so doing they supposedly sin against mercy. Thus, love for the different paradoxically excludes neighbors, even if faithful Catholics, and includes far-removed people, even unbelievers.

According to the new pastoral policy, this ironically discriminating welcoming helps accomplish a sort of mystical "emptying" (*kenosis*). In other words, the Church should be willing to divest herself of everything, not just by giving up prejudice towards the different, and renouncing all certainties and self-assurance, but also by marginalizing those faithful who dissent from that permissive stance. Their falling away will be offset precisely by the entry of various different types that will characterize the emerging "third Church" which will eventually replace the old, "Constantinian" or "Counter-Reformation" Church.

"Tear Down Walls and Build Bridges"

The commitment to welcome diversity presupposes the imperative of breaking down the barriers that still divide men; this imperative is summed up by the famous slogan, "tear down walls and build bridges."

In truth, breaking down walls of prejudice and distrust is the right thing to do. The Church has always done it, and that is why she is defined as Catholic, i.e. universal. But the new pastoral policy seems not to distinguish between provisional walls and protective ramparts, forgetting that walls can set boundaries protecting the peaceful from bullies. Therefore, it posits that walls inherently are factors of division, privilege, conflict and that it suffices to tear them down to do away with all enemies and wars. History proves the opposite, though; separation and distance often favor respect, protection, and peace not only within society but also the Church, like the massive walls that defended Jerusalem and its Temple for centuries, or those that still surround Vatican City.

It is likewise legitimate to build bridges as they favor communication between men. This is something the Church has always done as well, for example, by inventing the art of diplomacy. But the new pastoral policy forgets that bridges can become bridgeheads that allow bullies to break into our home. Furthermore, bridges can be used in two opposite directions: One running from the world to the Church, which favors conversion; or one going from the Church to the world, which encourages apostasy. Failure to distinguish between these two directions risks producing the illusion that the mere fact of building bridges fosters friendship, integration, communion, and peace. Recent history shows the contrary: Never before have men communicated so intensely; yet never before have they engaged in so many conflicts, to the point that recently built bridges seem to favor a global conflict.

Overcoming Discrimination Through Inclusion

The categorical imperative to break down walls is aimed at *overcoming discrimination through inclusion.*

By definition, discrimination means unequal treatment resulting from differing judgments. Therefore, it originally indicates a neutral method, the validity of which depends on whether or not the judgment issued conforms to truth and whether or not the treatment given conforms to justice. To discriminate means to judge things and people for what they are and according to their real worth, for example, by distinguishing right from wrong, or normal from abnormal, so as to "give everyone his due," which, as is well known, is the motto of distributive justice.

Conversely, advocates of the new pastoral policy tend

to argue that all discrimination that causes inequalities and exclusion must be condemned and overcome through inclusion. What was once discriminated as irregular or immoral must now be included on an equal footing and without conditions not only in society but also in the Church.

Obviously, this can also apply to irregular situations concerning marriage and the family. Not surprisingly, many governments have legalized divorce, homosexuality, abortion, and euthanasia on the pretext that social inclusion is now the revolutionary way to decide and govern, as some political authorities have recently admitted.

Marriage Through Intermediate Stages

An example of ecclesial integration that overcomes discrimination through inclusion is to admit *marriage through intermediate stages* as a concrete application of the principle of "gradualness of the [moral and canonical] law."

In the synodal debate, some bishops proposed that marriage can be accessed or returned to in stages. For example, the engaged couple can come to marriage by passing through intermediate stages of cohabitation and divorcees can resume the bond they feel more authentic. This would make it possible to ascertain whether the cohabiting partners are mature enough to commit to the final sacramental oath, to prevent marriages being celebrated hastily or wrongly, ending with separation or dissolution.

Now then, it is true that conversion from an illicit to a licit situation can occur along a path that gradually passes through intermediate stages. But this is admissible only if the stages of this journey of conversion are themselves morally licit, e.g. breaking up an illicit relationship or re-establishing a licit bond. By contrast, an illegal stage can in no way be accepted as if it were a temporary phase of Christian maturing and ecclesial integration; it is not enough for a stage to be partially or temporarily licit, not even for it to be *less illicit* than the previous one. For example, cohabitation *more uxorio* [like husband and wife] cannot be a legitimate step in a process assumed to end with marriage. "Nor can it ever involve the [priestly] blessing of these relations, lest confusion arise among the faithful concerning the value of marriage."[75]

At any rate, the Church's traditional teaching and pastoral policy have always excluded the licitness and legitimacy of both temporary and test marriages through gradual stages of coexistence. Sacramental marriage is valid only if the engaged couple gives their union an unconditional consent that immediately makes them spouses and allows no retraction.

> Some men go so far as to concoct new species of unions, suited, as they say, to the present temper of men and the times, which various new forms of matrimony they presume to label "temporary," "experimental," and "companionate." These offer all the indulgence of matrimony and its rights without, however, the indissoluble bond. . . . Indeed there are some who desire and insist that such abominations be legitimatized by the law or, at least, excused by their general acceptance among the people.[76]

---

75. Benedict XVI, Apostolic Exhortation, *Sacramentum caritatis*, Feb. 22, 2007, no. 29, http://w2.vatican.va/content/benedict-xvi/en/apost_exhortations /documents/hf_ben-xvi_exh_20070222_sacramentum-caritatis.html.

76. Pius XI, *Casti connubii*, nos. 51–2.

Quality in Emotional Relationships

The practice of marriage through intermediate stages presupposes that the new pastoral policy admit as morally licit cohabitation based on *emotional relationships* which, to be comparable to marriage, are said to have *quality.*

Having acknowledged that the licitness of unions comprises partially licit forms of cohabitation, the new pastoral policy of integration seems to conclude that, since society has superseded the old model of couple or family we must now accept a plurality of cohabitation types corresponding to the various emotional relationships and complex situations determined by the demands of modern life.

In the synodal debate, some bishops suggested recognizing civil unions (domestic partnerships) that enshrine forms of cohabitation different from traditional (heterosexual, monogamous and indissoluble) marriage. Such partnerships may be accepted as morally licit—they argued—provided they are based on quality emotional relationships, i.e. in which people commit to an authentic and stable union involving mutual material and moral support. In this view, marriage by stages, fornication, bigamy, polygamy, and even homosexual cohabitation, promoted as quality emotional relationships, would sooner or later become integrated into the pluralistic concept of marriage and enshrined in family law. But in acting under the illusion of raising cohabitation to the level of marriage, do we not end up by lowering the latter to match the former?

In fact, while a vague and misleading language attempts to dignify various forms of immoral cohabitation, heterosexual, monogamous, and indissoluble marriage is the only quality (sexual) relationship willed by God, according to morals, and recognized by the Church. It forms the family, basic cell of society and cradle of generational transmission. All other forms of emotional relationships are mere bonds of friendship that have nothing to do with sexuality and procreation or just lack the qualities necessary to be compared to the institution of marriage as willed by God. "Today, the need to avoid confusing marriage with other types of unions based on weak love is especially urgent. It is only the rock of total, irrevocable love between a man and a woman that can serve as the foundation on which to build a society that will become a home for all mankind."[77]

---

77. Benedict XVI, "Address to Members of the Pontifical John Paul II Institute for Studies on Marriage and Family," May 11, 2006, http://w2.vatican.va/content /benedict-xvi/en/speeches/2006/may/documents/hf_ben-xvi_spe_20060511 _istituto-gp-ii.html.

CONCLUSION

A Dangerous Anti-Language That Favors Confusion in the Church

As we have seen in this brief analysis, this constellation of talismanic words and slogans shows a convergent unity of meaning such as to constitute a newspeak (as George Orwell described in his famous novel, *1984*) or rather an anti-language that deserves the ancient prophetic rebuke, "for you have perverted the words of the living God!" (Jer. 23:36).

This language disseminates a new pastoral policy that favors a change of mentality and sensibility, instilling a new theology according to which what matters is not so much orthodoxy but an *orthopraxy* erected as a hermeneutic method to reinterpret the Gospel and reform the Church. Thus, the guidelines it proposes are not so much doctrinal or moral but sentimental, striving to achieve a fully worldly human promotion erroneously raised to a supernatural level and endowed with salvific power in order to be "faithful both to the Truth and to Life" (Maurice Blondel), "faithful both to Heaven and Earth" (Teilhard de Chardin), "faithful to both God and Man" (Karl Rahner). For example, they claim that a man can be a Christian (at least anonymously) without believing in the revealed Truth or respecting the Law of the Gospel: It suffices for him to have an implicit attitude of openness to the Absolute, communion with the Mystery, and solidarity with the Other.

However, in this way, faith is reduced to fideism,

morality to relativism, the Church to a human community, and all Christianity to anthropocentric naturalism with the danger of being sucked into a dialectical vortex leading from sentimentalism to subjectivism and finally to skeptical and sterile relativism, as Paul VI admonished.[78] For example, in the field of theology of the family, they end up omitting that the primary purpose of sexuality and procreation is to beget and raise children to grow the Church and join the Creator in Heaven to be happy with Him for all eternity.

If this is the present state of affairs, the language we have analyzed promotes cultural confusion and an *ideological transshipment* which, instead of attaining a pastoral conversion of the Church may effect an internal *revolution* in the Church, seriously threatening its unity and internal peace. This danger has ancient roots. More than a century ago, Pope Pius X lamented this, saying: "Modernists . . . cloak them [their errors] in certain ambiguous words and nebulous formulas to catch the incautious in their snares while always keeping open an escape route to avoid suffering outright condemnation."[79]

Later, improved techniques of linguistic and mass media manipulation at the service of anti-Christian psychological warfare have exacerbated the danger that the unwise employment of incorrect and misleading words can lead the faithful to drift away from the Catholic faith unsuspectingly.

A reader might object that the words and slogans we analyzed have become popular not only in the ecclesial community but also in recent Magisterium. We respond

---

78. See Paul VI, Letter *Lumen Ecclesiae*, Nov. 20, 1974, nos. 14–19, http://w2.vatican.va/content/paul-vi/it/letters/1974/documents /hf_p-vi_let_19741120_lumen-ecclesiae.html.

79. Pius X, "Address to the Cardinals," Apr. 17, 1907, http://w2.vatican.va/content /pius-x/it/speeches/documents/hf_p-x_spe_19070417_nuovi-cardinali.html.

with the words of theologian Fr. Louis Bouyer:

> The importance of the human factor in the exercise of the pastoral function . . . is very great. Here the Holy Spirit does not ensure an action *ex opere operato*. . . . Pastors at every hierarchical level can commit any and all errors of judgment or individual and collective sins in the exercise of pastoral authority or responsibility. Our only certainty is that the sins committed by human instruments of the Kingdom of Christ, though serious and numerous, will never be able to destroy the Church.[80]

At any rate, the current situation makes it more than ever necessary to observe the rule already established by Saint Augustine: "We [Christians] are bound to speak according to a certain rule, lest freedom of speech beget impiety of opinion about the matters themselves of which we speak."[81]

Only the linguistic reorganization advocated as far back as 1870 by the great Catholic sociologist Frédéric le Play makes this possible: "That which is difficult to obtain by employing defined words becomes easy when using vague words which, depending on the state of mind of those who read or hear them, comprise an absolutely opposed meaning.[82]

In short, it is now more necessary than ever to heed the well-known Gospel warning: "Let your speech be yea, yea: no, no: and that which is over and above these, is from the evil one" (Matt. 5:37).

---

80. Louis Bouyer, *L'Eglise* (Paris: Editions du Cerf, 1980), 500–1.

81. St. Augustine, *City of God*, bk. 10, ch. 23.

82. Frédéric Le Play, *L'organisation du travail* (Tours: Alfred Mame et fils, 1870), 336, http://gallica.bnf.fr/ark:/12148/bpt6k74343g/f4.image.

APPENDIX

Unperceived Ideological Transshipment: An Increasingly Relevant Issue

In his famous essay, *Unperceived Ideological Transshipment and Dialogue*, Plinio Corrêa de Oliveira wrote:

> The many meanings given to the word dialogue in certain circles have sounded false to our ears for some time. We have observed that in the daily speech of these circles and in certain press commentaries the word dialogue is used in an artificial and forced way around a fixed point of legitimate residual meaning. Furthermore, it is used in such disconcertingly daring ways and with so many underlying meanings that we felt an urgent need, as if dictated by conscience, to protest against such a flagrant violation of the rules of good speech.
>
> Little by little, the impressions, observations and notes we gathered here and there made us feel that the diversiform twisting of the word dialogue had an underlying consistency that appeared to be something intentional, methodical and planned. In addition, we had the feeling that, besides dialogue, this included other words.[83]

While stressing that, originally, those words had an

---

83. Corrêa de Oliveira, *Unperceived Ideological Transshipment*, intro. 1.

absolutely legitimate meaning, the Brazilian thinker stated that when they are used in a certain context, they form a kind of "constellation of talismans" that is specifically used to create a psychological effect on people, tending to bring about a profound transformation of their mentalities. He defines this process with an expression that has deservedly become famous: unperceived ideological transshipment.

The author published this essay in 1965, at the apex of the Cold War. The immediate purpose of his analysis of the effect of certain talismanic words was to demonstrate that they served to "weaken the resistance of non-communists by giving their souls a propensity towards condescension, sympathy, non-resistance, or even surrender. In extreme cases, this twisting even succeeded in transforming non-communists into communists."[84]

After mentioning the Marxists' faltering efforts and historical failure in their dissemination of Marxist theories and even military coups to seize power and gain public support, the essay shows how it became indispensable for communist leaders to resort to *psychological warfare*, which included the use of *talismanic words* to carry out an *unperceived ideological transshipment* that would lead ordinary people to accept, in one way or another, what they had repudiated before.

The essay's relevance today is not in its description of the strategy of communist expansion as it existed before the implosion of the Soviet world (that now belongs to history), but in the description and analysis of the technique of unperceived ideological transshipment, which can be used by any movement, party, or lobby to

---

84. Ibid.

win over public opinion in general or a particular segment of opinion such as, for example, Catholic, European, middle-class opinion, etc. A brief summary will show how, instead of losing its interest, the topic has become more and more relevant and applicable to the present reality.

In this quick overview of the essay, we propose to capture and describe the essence of Plinio Corrêa de Oliveira's theses using his words, whenever feasible. Thus we will try to leave out historical circumstances of the time as described by the author. In so doing, we hope to make it easier for the reader to concentrate his attention on the *psywar* strategy, which has become increasingly sophisticated and effective in these early years of the third millennium.

In the sixties, the author identifies the word *dialogue* as a typical term with *talismanic* effects and devotes a substantial part of his essay to its analysis. While it can be used correctly, the term dialogue continues to serve as a talismanic word in certain contexts. And this, despite the fact that, over time, a whole new constellation of talismanic words and expressions has been developing which is capable of producing effects that go far beyond their immediate and natural meaning.

There is nothing reprehensible as such about other talismanic words, like *peace*, or *coexistence*; to affirm as much would be an aberration. However, the essay does not make "a preliminary study of [their] natural and legitimate meanings," but only "show[s] in which of them evolution towards the first talismanic meaning occurs,"[85] making them useful tools to carry out a strategy. The

---

85. Ibid., ch. 4, 1.

same can and must be said of the talismanic words and expressions that are discussed in this book.

The Need for Implicit Action

A first observation Plinio Corrêa de Oliveira makes is that a majority of people showed themselves refractory to the *explicit* preaching of Marxist ideas, forcing the use of an *implicit* action. This implicit action is exercised on the average person, the man-in-the-street, whom the essay likens to a medical *patient*. "In varying degrees of clarity, they [the patients] know that they are 'evolving' ideologically. But it seems to them that this evolution is a process in which they themselves are gradually discovering or deepening their knowledge of an appealing 'truth,' or constellation of 'truths,' without the aid of anyone else."[86]

Accordingly, during almost the entire process these patients never realize that they are increasingly distancing themselves ideologically from their original position, and "if at a certain moment this danger were made apparent to them, they would *ipso facto* recognize the abyss into which they are falling and would step back." They will notice it only at the end of the process, "but at this point, their mentality has so 'evolved' that the hypothesis of becoming adherents of communism no longer horrifies but rather attracts them."[87]

The Role of Language in Ideological Evolution

Insisting that what the author says of communism can be applied by analogy to multiple processes of unperceived

---

86. Ibid., intro. 3.

87. Ibid.

ideological transshipment, let us see what he says:

> We call this phenomenon ... unperceived
> ideological transshipment. We propose to
> succinctly describe its essential aspects and,
> since it is used in different ways, to study es-
> pecially its application in what we call the
> stratagem of the talismanic word....
>
> The phenomenon of unperceived ideolog-
> ical transshipment has various modalities. It
> can either develop in all its fullness and rad-
> icality by leading the patient all the way to ac-
> cepting communism or take on a less ample
> and radical mode, e.g. when its victim merely
> becomes socialist instead of communist....
>
> This process also may be directed only at
> theories and methods of action, rather than
> at a whole philosophical conception of the
> universe, of life, man, culture, economics, so-
> ciology, and politics, such as Marxism.[88]

To illustrate his point, the author begins by examining
the impasse in which communism found itself at the time.
In fact, communists concluded that neither the action of
intellectuals nor the violence of guns had gained the common people's favor and sympathy for their ideology. Inci-
dentally, this phenomenon has continued toward other
spreading ideologies which, while not resorting to violence, were supported by the great cultural, political circles, and mass media, but nevertheless failed to capture
the mind of the average man. The common denominator
between what happened to classic communism and what
now happens to other ideologies is that, after a promising
start, they always end up more or less stagnant. In other

---

88. Ibid., intro. 4.

words, after an initial period in which they manage to attract a limited group of people, in the medium and long term, they are unable to change the persuasions of a wider swath of public opinion.

That is when it becomes essential to apply *implicit action* using renewed, twisted, and distorted semantics.

At this point, our readers can make the necessary adaptations to today's changed historical circumstances, for example, by replacing what was written about communism with theological neo-modernism or the secularist ideology that seeks to modify the natural concept of the family. They will easily see how relevant and important the issue is.

Who Are the Patients of Unperceived Ideological Transshipment?

Plinio Corrêa de Oliveira writes:

> In order to get a precise focus on what unperceived ideological transshipment is, we must first show how, as a method of persuasion, it differs from the "classical" methods of a Communist Party....
>
> As a rule, a Communist Party is formed with a nucleus of intellectuals or semi-intellectuals who stir up or exploit various factors of discontent and agitation. This is done through well-known methods—individual recruiting in universities, unions, armed forces and so on, lectures and speeches, the press, radio, television, theater and the cinema. Once the climate has been prepared, the initial handful of adepts begins to expound communist doctrine openly. Sometimes bold,

sometimes cautious, they will do so immediately or wait according to circumstances. This
indoctrination forms a group of fanaticized recruits. The party is established; during this
first phase it stirs up, stimulates, and recruits
all the "Bolshevizable" people in the circles in
which it is acting, people who are predisposed
to adhere to communism on account of multiple ideological, moral, and economic factors.

But experience shows that after a time
these first and sometimes rapid successes of
the Marxist technique of persuasion stop.
Once the "Bolshevizables" of a certain circle
are recruited.... But they are normally a mi-
nority ... [and] its propaganda collides with
an unresponsive majority.... How can communism conquer this majority?

To answer this question, one must first realize that this majority is made up of three
different types of people: those in some
measure sympathetic to communism, those
categorically opposed to it, and those only
vaguely opposed to it who do nothing.

Communist strategy is appropriately
adapted to each one of these types.[89]

Communist mentors try to exploit those in the first
category as useful idiots and fellow travelers as long as
they are helpful to their cause, which seeks to overthrow
a certain order of things. "Once this result is obtained,
these unfortunate accomplices will be cast aside, perse-
cuted and destroyed if they do not join the Communist
Party immediately and subject themselves to it without

---

89. Ibid., ch. 2, 1–2.

reservation."[90]

Communists find it necessary to work on those who are categorically hostile and even militantly against communism "with a total psychological offensive aiming at disorganizing, discouraging and reducing them to inaction."[91] This is done in such a way as to make them

> feel spied upon both inside and outside their organizations, surrounded by traitors, divided among themselves, misunderstood, defamed and isolated from other currents of opinion, excluded from the country's key positions and means of publicity, and so persecuted in their professional activities that, having barely enough time to provide for their own subsistence, they are prevented from effectively acting against Marxism. . . .
>
> The majority within the majority, so to speak, is made up of people indifferent to the problem of communism, unfriendly to it in different degrees, but who have no militant hostility toward it. Since they show themselves intractable to every technique of explicit persuasion, communism is left with only one way to attract them: the technique of *implicit persuasion.* Naturally, for this operation to be possible, the communist party must stay out of sight. It has to pick agents posing as non-communists or even as anti-communists to act in the various sectors of society. The less they are suspected of being communists, the more efficient they are likely to be. On the level of individual activism, for

---

90. Ibid., ch. 2, 2.

91. Ibid.

example, a prominent capitalist, an important local politician, an aristocrat or a priest are much more useful than a simple merchant or a laborer.

Much can be done in favor of communism in this sector of public opinion through political parties, newspapers, and other means of publicity which appear absolutely unaffected by communism but do not focus on the struggle against it as a necessity of continued and capital importance.

Such persons, political parties, and media lend a prime and precious cooperation to communism simply by maintaining a climate of superficiality and an easy and carefree optimism.... This atmosphere makes anti-communist organizations appear emotional and extremist to the greater part of the public that could and should support them. Furthermore, the failure to warn the public about the present seriousness of the communist danger prevents the indifferent from becoming antagonistic to communism and the non-militant anti-communists from entering the fight. These two results are precious to Marxism....

This is a considerable accomplishment but it is not enough for communism. Unable to conquer this majority, communism lulls it to sleep; as long as it is unable to conquer it, communism will be forced to advance slowly. And, if some day this advance matures and becomes undisguisable, that inattentive and distracted majority might be jolted out of its slumber and join the fight....

These are the same majorities that communism must persuade, more than neutralize, to win its great battle in our times.[92]

But how to do it? "Unperceived ideological transship-ment is the technique of implicit persuasion most suited to the state of mind of today's majority."[93]

Unperceived Ideological Transshipment and its Tricks

Essentially, the process of unperceived ideological transshipment consists in act-ing upon someone's mind to make him change his ideology without perceiving it.

Several different artifices can be used to obtain this result. Usually, these arti-fices are:

a) Finding, in the ideological system the patient currently accepts, points of affinity with the desired ideological system;

b) Over-emphasizing those points of affin-ity, from the standpoint of doctrine and emo-tion, so that the patient puts them above all the other ideological values he accepts;

c) De-emphasizing as much as possible the patient's adhesion to doctrinal princi-ples which might be irreconcilable with the ideology to which he is being transshipped;

d) Attracting the patient's sympathy for the militants and leaders of the desired ideological movement, making him see them as soldiers of the over-emphasized principles in item "b";

e) To go from this sympathy to cooperation in achieving goals common to the patient and

92. Ibid. (Our emphasis.)
93. Ibid.

his former doctrinal adversaries, or to fight an ideology or a current of opinion inimical to both;

f) Thence giving the patient the conviction that the over-emphasized principles are more consistent with the ideology of his new friends and brothers in the struggle than with his former ideology;

g) At this point, the patient's mentality will have been changed, and his assimilation by the new ideology will only encounter secondary obstacles.

During nearly this whole process, the patient:

— will not realize that his ideas are changing, and when he finally does realize it, he won't be frightened;

— imagines that he is acting on his own from start to finish, unconscious that he is being maneuvered.

Thus, he is gradually transformed from an adversary into a sympathizer and finally a follower.[94]

According to the author, in order to succeed it becomes of paramount importance to excite the patient's emotions by stirring up in him an unbalanced desire for an abstract value such as, for example, human brotherhood, to the point of making him simplistically believe that the solution to the world's problems is the establishment of a multicultural, multi-religious, and multi-ethnic Universal Republic. The more this emotion grows, the easier it will be to paint every inequality and discrimination

94. Ibid., ch. 2, 4.

as obstacles to be removed, recognizing a need to combat them at the legislative level, through profound structural and institutional reforms. With the laudable pretext of eliminating unjust inequalities, they will often also abolish distinctions that are necessary for human dignity and the attainment of the common good.

The Talismanic Word

Historically, the talismanic word has shown to be the most effective means to produce unperceived ideological transshipment. This technique shows the absolute relevance today of Plinio Corrêa de Oliveira's study, as the changes we are witnessing in contemporary thinking, sometimes passed off as inevitable anthropological changes in the wake of neo-Darwinian theories, actually correspond to a clearly articulated ideological operation that uses new and efficient talismanic words and expressions.

Let us follow the author's reasoning:

> At this initial position, in which the patient is . . . already prepared for the psychological action that he is about to undergo, the use of a well-chosen word can produce surprising effects. This word is the talismanic word.
>
> This is a word whose legitimate meaning is congenial and, at times, even noble; but it is also a word that has some elasticity. When it is used tendentiously, it begins to shine with a new radiance, fascinating the patient and taking him much farther than he could have imagined.
>
> Twisted out of shape and distorted, wholesome and even dignified words have been used to label a number of mistakes, errors

and blunders. We could even say that the effects of this technique are more harmful when the word being abused is more elevated and dignified— *corruptio optimi pessima*. Some words with a dignified connotation that have been transformed into deceitful talismans and placed at the service of error are: social justice, ecumenism, dialogue, peace, irenicism, and coexistence. . . .

Thus charged with a new spirit, each of these words raises up a network of impressions, emotions, sympathies, and phobias in persons with the states of mind described in items A and B. As shown below, this network orients the victims toward new ideological directions: philosophical relativism, religious syncretism, socialism, the policy of the extended hand, open cooperation with communism and finally, the acceptance of Marxist doctrine. . . .

The prestige of propaganda leads the victim of the transshipment process to become more and more attracted to these new ideological paths. The talismanic words correspond to what the media generally considers modern, pleasant and attractive. Thus, the lecturers, speakers, or writers who use these words do so for the sole reason of seeing their chances of a good reception in the press, radio, or television considerably enhanced. For this reason the person listening to the radio or the television or reading the newspaper will find these words used everywhere in every possible way, with growing repercussion in his soul. . . .

The propagandistic quality of the talismanic word leads the writer, speaker, and lecturer to the temptation of using it with increasing frequency for every application, and even when it is not applicable, thus making himself more easily applauded. And in order to increase the opportunities of using such words, he uses them in analogous and successively broader ways, stretching their natural elasticity almost to absurdity. . . .

With such a great range of uses for the talismanic word, the bolder uses cause the more moderate, sensible, and current ones to fall into disuse. Those who formerly would use the talismanic word with a slightly deformed meaning, or applaud its use as if it were a new plaything, will begin to applaud and use it in more and more exaggerated senses, until it reaches a climax. This is the phenomenon of the radicalization of the talismanic word. . . .

This very process of radicalizing the talismanic word causes the unperceived ideological transshipment of those who use it. Fascinated by the word, they quickly accept as supreme and ardently professed ideals the successively more radical meanings that it assumes.

With the force of values accepted as supreme, these ideals in turn gradually produce in the victim of the transshipment process all the interior and exterior changes of attitude toward his former adversary described in the previous chapter.

This is how the talismanic word is used to unleash the process of unperceived ideological transshipment and bring it to a close.[95]

---

95. Ibid., ch. 3, 2, C-H.

At this point, the author says, to eradicate the subliminal effect of the transshipment process, an explanation of the process will have an "exorcistic" effect on the talismanic word, whose "real power lies in the emotion which it excites"[96] rather than in its natural meaning. Hence, "reflection, drawing toward the talismanic word the analytic attention of whoever uses or hears it, would disturb and impede *ipso facto* the sensible and imaginative fruition of the word. By keeping its meaning obstinately implicit, the talismanic word continues to be a vehicle and a hiding place for its increasing emotional content."[97]

Obviously, "we are not suggesting here that one should never use a word with talismanic meaning, but simply that it be used **properly** and always in its natural and legitimate sense."[98]

Dialogue, an Example of a Talismanic Word

Plinio Corrêa de Oliveira devotes the remainder of his essay to make a detailed analysis of a striking example of a talismanic word used in unperceived ideological transshipment: the word *dialogue*, which is still effective today when used with a talismanic meaning.

From its etymological and legitimate meaning—which includes all possible forms of human dialogue, from mere entertainment conversation to more or less energetic discussion and polemics—the word can be stretched to take on a connotation whereby dialoguing becomes something that sounds very noble and humane, destined almost exclusively to secure an interlocutor's

---

96. Ibid., ch. 3, 3, A.

97. Ibid.

98. Ibid., ch. 3, 4.

goodwill, even at the cost of concealing one's strongest convictions. "The word dialogue is reclothed in magic and fascinating scintillations when used in this perspective. Like a real talisman it automatically endows those who use it with its prestige and brilliance."[99]

With acumen, the author successively describes the various steps in which the term is used so as to increasingly distort its original and legitimate meaning, transshipping the patient from an uncompromising mindset on certain principles (non-negotiable principles, we would call them today) to the extreme opposite, a mentality aimed at relativizing, and hence bargaining truth away, sacrificing it in the hope of reaching an era of good will, peace, and universal brotherhood.

At what price can all that be attained?

At the price of rejecting the objective existence of truth and error, good and bad, concepts more clearly identified with an intellectual assertiveness that takes on a negative character and can drag men to controversy and possibly even violent confrontation.

Thus, by adopting the irenicist approach that undergirds belief in an era of good will people refrain from contrasting evil with good, something which Saint Thomas Aquinas teaches is needed to make the splendor of truth and good stand out as it should.[100]

In turn, Plinio Corrêa de Oliveira notes that "one thus inevitably slips toward confusion, which is one of the deepest and most sinister causes of disturbances, quarrels, and prolonged, inextricable and hateful

---

99. Ibid., ch.4, 3, C, d.

100. See St. Thomas Aquinas, *Summa contra gentiles*, trans. Vernon J. Bourque (New York: Hanover House, 1955), bk. III, q. 71. Online Edition rev. and ed. Joseph Kenny, O.P., http://dhspriory.org/thomas/ContraGentiles3a.htm#71.

fights."[101] Paradoxically, the irenicist path leads even more easily to confrontation. He also concluded that except for adopting an extreme utopia, dialogue could never completely replace the militant character of the Catholic Church, grounded on the "*inimicitias ponam*" of Genesis (3:15) and confirmed as a constant both in Church doctrine and in her 2,000-year history. "Emotional, ideological, or volitional clashes are, in themselves, fruits of original sin. It would be ideal if there never were dissensions."[102] Nevertheless, they are inevitable in human reality.

The Fear-Sympathy Syndrome

The more engaging, smiling, and Hegelian aspect of irenicist dialogue lies in the average man's worldly and optimistic desire of placing all his hopes in the earthly reality and almost instinctively shunning the crosses of life. On the other hand, the worldly man is afraid to embark on a path that eventually leads from controversy to dissension and beyond. At that point he psychologically opens up to talismanic dialogue, moved by one of the most powerful triggers of unperceived ideological transshipment: the *fear-sympathy syndrome.*

During the Cold War, the fear-sympathy syndrome worked by craftily flashing before the eyes of the Western bourgeoisie the somewhat fallacious alternative of either a nuclear war that would annihilate mankind or an accommodating dialogue that ushered in the long-awaited era of good will. The fear-sympathy syndrome mechanism which drives ideological transshipment is renewed

---

101. Corrêa de Oliveira, *Unperceived Ideological Transshipment*, ch.4, 1, D, h.

102. Ibid., ch. 4, 1, D. a.

with changing historical circumstances and always finds new elements to advance the process. For example, we could say that today we are faced with another false dilemma: To not antagonize the fear-inducing cutthroats it is best to relinquish any claims of ideals or religious identity and continue living in a peaceful multicultural society, in which, hopefully, we can hold on to much of our lifestyle.

A Paradox: Opponents Become Friends, and Friends, Opponents

At first, those subjected to the ideology of appeasing and irenicistic dialogue begin to find their one-time opponents more and more likable and, simultaneously, those whose ideals and principles they once shared become increasingly unpopular to the point of being excluded as much as possible from personal relationships and social influence. Indeed, in the new era of good will, patients of ideological transshipment see those who adamantly cling to the principles they once affirmed as party spoilers while their admiration and confidence in their former opponents grow. Back in 1965, Plinio Corrêa de Oliveira already saw that process causing a "constantly increasing decimation among the most ardent sons of the Church Militant."[103]

But this is not the only consequence of the ideological transshipment process. As seen above, it also leads to the radicalization of a mentality which, having started from an irenicist emotionality, slides to philosophical and moral relativism. There is an interaction, the author says, "between the irenicistic emotion and

---

103. Ibid., ch. 4, 3, C, b.

the talismanic word."[104] As this interaction develops, "the forms and contents of the interlocution between persons of opposite convictions are processively modified, correspondingly modifying also the meaning of the talismanic word. . . . The irenicistic interlocutor, gripped by the hidden content of the talismanic word—the irenic myth—uses the talismanic word for everything like a toy whose enchantment grows as he plays with it."[105] So, in extreme cases, that ideological transshipment which had "an ardent emotional desire for universal concord" can turn into a "completely irenical and relativistic conception of man, life and the cosmos . . . potentially conquered by irenicism in favor of relativism, and . . . its most radical form, Hegelian relativism." [106]

Toward Radical Relativism

How could that happen?

It could (and in fact does) happen because dialogue so understood "does not aim principally to obtain truth, and through that, unity; now it seeks mainly unity through cordiality in relations between the speakers. The conquest of truth through argument is only secondary."[107] Any intention to persuade that might dispel doctrinal "misunderstandings"[108] becomes disorderly and dangerous. At this point, the original and legitimate meaning of the word dialogue is completely changed for the benefit of an irenicist view of things.

---

104. Ibid., ch. 4, 3, D, b.

105. Ibid. ch. 4, 3, D, b, Second Phase.

106. Ibid. ch. 4, 3, D, b, First Phase.

107. Ibid.

108. Ibid., ch. 4, 3, C, b.

Indeed, this is Hegel's vision. "Dialogue begins to be practiced as a *ludus* [game] in which both parties admit that decantation of the truth will take place through dialogue, just as the clash of thesis and antithesis produces synthesis."[109] In this way, "truth . . . comes to be seen as a product of an eternal dialectic"[110] which is "contrary to the 'antipathetic' and 'discriminatory' manner of medieval Thomism [and] this distillation would neither condemn nor exclude anything."[111]

Consequence of Unperceived Ideological Transshipment for Catholics

Plinio Corrêa de Oliveira concludes that "the acceptance of a relativistic philosophy amounts to a conscious or subconscious break with the Faith, and it prepares the soul for the explicit profession of atheism."[112] And this because it reduces the doctrine of the Church to relative truths intended to dialectically confront other truths in search for a new synthesis which, in turn, will have to face new challenges posed by the history of human evolution. Apart from its dramatic final result—the spread of atheism— even now such a philosophical attitude throws Catholics "into a state of absolute confusion."[113]

> *Dialogue, coexistence,* and *peace* as talismanic words are used enigmatically in many circumstances. But if interpreted in an evolutionist and Hegelian sense, the enigmatic

---

109. Ibid. ch. 4, 3, D, b, Fourth Phase.

110. Ibid.

111. Ibid.

112. Ibid, concl., 1.

113. Ibid.

character is dissipated and these talismanic terms become clear, precise, and perfectly harmonious with each other. Now this presents us with a transshipping action of not just the one word *dialogue*, but of a whole world of similar talismanic words.[114]

This constellation of similar talismanic words can work in different fields of human activity, not just in the strictly philosophical one, for example, but also in the theological realm when it comes to carrying out the transshipment of the faithful.

---

114. Ibid., concl., 7.

BIBLIOGRAPHY

Alphonsus Ligouri, Saint. *Preparation for Death*. Boston: Thomas Sweeney, 1854.

Augustine, Saint. *The City of God*. Trans. Marcus Dods. *In Nicene and Post-Nicene Fathers*, 1st Series, Vol. 2. Ed. Philip Schaff. Buffalo, NY: Christian Literature Publishing Co., 1887. Rev. and ed. Kevin Knight for New Advent. http://www.newadvent.org/fathers/120121.htm.
———. Letter 211. Trans. J.G. Cunningham. In *Nicene and Post-Nicene Fathers*, 1st Series, Vol. 1. Ed. Philip Schaff. Buffalo, NY: Christian Literature Publishing Co., 1887. Rev. and ed. Kevin Knight for New Advent. http://www.newadvent.org/fathers/1102211.htm.
———. *Confessions*. Trans. J.G. Pilkington. In *Nicene and Post-Nicene Fathers*, 1st Series, Vol. 1. Ed. Philip Schaff. Buffalo, NY: Christian Literature Publishing Co., 1887. Rev. and ed. Kevin Knight for New Advent. http://www.newadvent.org/fathers/1101.htm.
———. *Homily 7 on the First Epistle of John*. Trans. H. Browne. In *Nicene and Post-Nicene Fathers*, 1st Series, Vol. 7. Ed. Philip Schaff. Buffalo, NY: Christian Literature Publishing Co., 1888. Rev. and ed. Kevin Knight for New Advent. http://www.newadvent.org/fathers/170207.htm.
———. *Homily 8 on the First Epistle of John*. Trans. H. Browne. In *Nicene and Post-Nicene Fathers*, 1st Series, Vol. 7. Ed. Philip Schaff. Buffalo, NY: Christian Literature Publishing Co., 1888. Rev. and ed. Kevin Knight for New Advent. http://www.newadvent.org/fathers/170208.htm.
———. *Homily 9 on the First Epistle of John*. Trans. H. Browne. In *Nicene and Post-Nicene Fathers*, 1st Series, Vol. 7. Ed. Philip Schaff. Buffalo, NY: Christian Literature Publishing Co., 1888. Rev. and ed. Kevin Knight for New Advent. http://www.newadvent.org/fathers/170209.htm.
———. *Sermones ad populum*.

Benedict XVI. "Address to the Participants in the Ecclesial Diocesan Convention of Rome." Jun. 6, 2005. http://w2.vatican.va/content/benedict-vi/en/speeches/2005/june/documents/hf_ben-xvi_spe_20050606_convegno-famiglia.html.

———. "La pastorale del matrimonio deve fondarsi sulla
    verita." *Osservatore Romano*. Nov. 30, 2011.
    http://www.osservatoreromano.va/it/news/la-pastorale-del-
    matrimonio-deve-fondarsi-sulla-ve.
———. Apostolic Exhortation *Sacramentum caritatis*. Feb. 22,
    2007. http://w2.vatican.va/content/benedict-xvi/en/apost
    _exhortations/documents/hf_ben-xvi_exh_20070222
    _sacramentum-caritatis.html.
———. "Address to Members of the Pontifical John Paul II Institute
    for Studies on Marriage and Family." May 11, 2006.
    http://w2.vatican.va/content/benedict-xvi/en/speeches
    /2006/may/documents/hf_ben-xvi_spe_20060511_istituto
    -gp-ii.html.

Bonaventure, Saint. *In Secundum Librum Sententiarum*. In *Doctoris
    seraphici S. Bonaventurae Opera Omnia*, Vol. II. Florence: Ty-
    pographia Collegii S. Bonaventurae, 1885. http://www.archive.org
    /stream/doctorisseraphic02bona#page/906/mode/2up.

Bouyer, Louis. *L'Eglise*. Paris: Editions du Cerf, 1980.

Catechism of the Catholic Church. Cita del Vaticano: Libreria Ed-
    itrice Vaticana, 2003. http://www.vatican.va/archive/ENG0015
    /_INDEX.HTM.

Catechism of the Council of Trent. Accessed Mar. 5, 2017.
    http://www.catholicbook.com/AgredaCD/Trent/tcreed12.htm.

Corrêa de Oliveira, Plinio. *Unperceived Ideological Transshipment
    and Dialogue*. Oct. 1, 1982. http://www.tfp.org/tfp-home/books
    /unperceived-ideological-transshipment-and-dialogue.html.

*Didache—The Lord's Teaching Through the Twelve Apostles to the
    Nations*. Trans. M.B. Riddle. In *Ante-Nicene Fathers*, Vol. 7. Ed.
    Alexander Roberts, et. al. Buffalo, NY: Christian Literature
    Publishing Co., 1886. Rev. and ed. Kevin Knight for New Ad-
    vent. http://www.newadvent.org /fathers/0714.htm.

Francis. "Homily During Mass with the New Cardinals." Feb. 15, 2015. http://w2.vatican.va/content/francesco/en/homilies/2015 /documents/papa-francesco_20150215_omelia-nuovi -cardinali.html.

———. Apostolic Exhortation *Evangelii Gaudium.* Nov. 24, 2013. http://w2.vatican.va/content/francesco/en/apost _exhortations/documents/papa-francesco_esortazione- ap_20131124_evangelii-gaudium.html.

Gregory the Great, Saint. *Pastoral Care.* Trans. James Barmby. In *Nicene and Post-Nicene Fathers*, 2nd Series, Vol. 12. Ed. Philip Schaff and Henry Wace. Buffalo, NY: Christian Literature Pub- lishing Co., 1895. Rev. and ed. Kevin Knight for New Advent. http://www.newadvent.org/fathers/36011.htm.

Guitton, Jean. *Paul VI segreto.* Cinisello Balsamo, Italy: Ed. San Paolo, 2002.

Huby, SJ, Joseph. *San Paolo: Epistole della prigionia.* Rome: Studium, 1960.

Le Play, Frédéric. *L'organisation du travail.* Tours: Alfred Mame et fils, 1870. http://gallica.bnf.fr/ark:/12148/bpt6k74343g/f4.image.

Janvier, OP, Emile. *Esposizione della morale cattolica.* Turin: Marietti, 1936.

John Paul II. "Speech to the Participants of the International Con- gress on Moral Theology." Apr. 10, 1986. http://w2.vatican.va /content/john-paul-ii/it/speeches/1986/april/documents/hf_jp -ii_spe_19860410_teologia-morale.html.

———. Encyclical *Dives in misericordia.* Nov. 30, 1980. http://w2.vatican.va/content/john-paul-ii/en/encyclicals /documents/hf_jp-ii_enc_30111980_dives-in -misericordia.html.

———. Apostolic Exhortation *Familiaris consortio.* Nov. 22, 1981. http://w2.vatican.va/content/john-paul-ii/en/apost _exhortations/documents/hf_jp-ii_exh_19811122_familiaris -consortio.html.

————. Encyclical *Redemptoris Missio*. Dec. 7, 1990.
   http://w2.vatican.va/content/john-paul-ii/en/encyclicals
   /documents/hf_jp-ii_enc_07121990_redemptoris-missio.html.
————. Encyclical *Slavorum apostoli*. Jun. 2, 1985.
   http://w2.vatican.va/content/john-paul-ii/en/encyclicals
   /documents/hf_jp-ii_enc_19850602_slavorum-apostoli.html.
————. Encyclical *Veritatis Splendor*. Aug. 6, 1993.
   http://w2.vatican.va/content/john-paul-ii/en/encyclicals
   /documents/hf_jp-ii_enc_06081993_veritatis-splendor.html.

Marx, Karl. *Theses on Feuerbach*. Accessed Mar. 14, 2017.
   https://msuweb.montclair.edu/~furrg/gned/marxtonf45.pdf.

Menander of Athens. *Monosticha*. Quoted in W. Gurney Benham.
   Cassell's Book of Quotations. Revised edition. New York: Cassell
   and Company, Ltd., 1914.

Pagotto, Aldo di Cillo, Robert F. Vasa, and Athanasius Schneider.
   *Preferential Option for the Family: One Hundred Questions and
   Answers Relating to the Synod*. Rome: Edizioni Supplica Filiale,
   2015. http://www.tfp.org/images/stories/PDF_files/Preferential
   _Option_for_the_Family_English.pdf.

Paul VI. "General Audience." Feb. 12, 1969. http://w2.vatican.va
   /content/paul-vi/it/audiences/1969/documents/hf_p
   -vi_aud_19690212.html.
————. Letter *Lumen Ecclesiae*. Nov. 20, 1974.
   http://w2.vatican.va/content/paul-vi/it/letters/1974
   /documents/hf_p-vi_let_19741120_lumen-ecclesiae.html.
————. Apostolic Exhortation *Evangelii nuntiand*. Dec. 8, 1975.
   http://w2.vatican.va/content/paul-vi/en/apost
   _exhortations/documents/hf_p-vi_exh_19751208
   _evangelii-nuntiandi.html.
————. "Closing Allocution for the III General Assembly of the
   Synod of Bishops." Oct. 26, 1974. http://w2.vatican.va
   /content/paul-vi/it/speeches/1974/documents
   /hf_p-vi_spe_19741026_allocuzione-finale.html.

Pieper, Josef. *Faith Hope Love*. San Francisco: Ignatius Press, 1997.
    Original English edition: Pieper. Josef. *About Love*. Translated
    by Richard and Clara Winston. Chicago: Franciscan Herald
    Press, 1974.

Pindar, *Pythian II*. Translated and edited by Diane Arnson Svarlien.
    From *The Odes of Pindar*, in *Perseus Project* 1.0. New Haven:
    Yale University Press, 1991. http://www.perseus.tufts.edu.

Pius VII. Brief *Etsi fraternitatis*. Aug. 10, 1803.

Pius IX. *Syllabus of Errors*. Dec. 8, 1864. http://www.ewtn.com
    /library/PAPALDOC/P9SYLL.HTM.

Pius X. "Address to the Cardinals." Apr. 17, 1907.
    http://w2.vatican.va/content/pius-x/it/speeches/documents
    /hf_p-x_spe_19070417_nuovi-cardinali.html.

Pius XI. Encyclical *Casti connubii*. Dec. 31, 1930.
    https://w2.vatican.va/content/pius-xi/en/encyclicals
    /documents/hf_p-xi_enc_19301231_casti-connubii.html.

Pius XII. "Speech to the Cardinals and Bishops in Rome for the
    Proclamation of the Dogma of the Assumption of the Blessed
    Virgin Mary." Nov. 2, 1950. http://w2.vatican.va/content
    /pius-xii/la/speeches/1950/documents/hf_p
    -xii_spe_19501102_episcopato-mondo-cattolico.html.
    ———. "Speech to the Pontifical Mission Societies." June 24, 1944.
    http://w2.vatican.va/content/pius-xii/it/speeches/1944
    /documents/hf_p-xii_spe_19440624_opere-missionarie.html.

Ratzinger, Joseph Cardinal, with Vittorio Messori. *The Ratzinger
    Report: An Exclusive Interview on the State of the Church*. Trans-
    lated by Salvator Attanasio and Graham Harrison. San Fran-
    cisco: Ignatius Press, 1985.
    ———. *To Look on Christ: Exercises in Faith, Hope, and Love*. n.p.:
    Crossroad Pub. Co., 1991.

Ries, Julien. "Inculturazione." In Poupard, Cardinal Paul.
    Dizionario delle religioni. Rome: Città Nuova, 2001.

Royo Marin, OP, Antonio. *Teologia de la Caridad*. Madrid: B.A.C., 1960.

Shakespeare, William. *Hamlet*. Edited by Hardin Craig. *The Complete Works of Shakespeare*. Chicago: Scott, Foreman and Co., 1961.

Spadaro, Antonio. *La famiglia oltre il miraggio: Tutti i documenti del Sinodo straordinario 2015*. Milan-Rome: Ancora/La Civiltà Cattolica, 2015.

Thomas Aquinas, Saint. *Summa contra gentiles*. Trans. Vernon J. Bourque. New York: Hanover House, 1955. Online Edition rev. and ed. Joseph Kenny, O.P. http://dhspriory.org/thomas /ContraGentiles3a.htm#71.
———. *Summa Theologiae*. Trans. Fathers of the English Dominican Province. London: Burns and Oates, 1920. Rev. and ed. Kevin Knight for New Advent. http://www.newadvent.org/summa /3060.htm.

Zoffoli C.P., Enrico. *Dizionario del Cristianesimo*. Rome: Synopsis, 1992.

This work is available as a free e-book at:
www.TFP.org/PastoralRevolution